A Guy's Guide to Dating

Everything You Need to Know

About Love, SEX,

Relationships, and

Other Things *Too Terrible*

to Contemplate

Brendan Baber

and

Eric Spitznagel

a GUY'S GUIDE *to*

Dating

MAIN STREET BOOKS

Doubleday

New York • London • Toronto • Sydney • Auckland

A MAIN STREET BOOK
PUBLISHED BY DOUBLEDAY
a division of Bantam Doubleday Dell Publishing Group, Inc.
1540 Broadway, New York, New York 10036

MAIN STREET BOOKS, DOUBLEDAY, and the portrayal of a building
with a tree are trademarks of Doubleday, a division of Bantam
Doubleday Dell Publishing Group, Inc.

BOOK DESIGN BY JUDITH STAGNITTO ABBATE

Library of Congress Cataloging-in-Publication Data

Baber, Brendan.
A guy's guide to dating: everything you need to know about love,
sex, relationships, and other things too terrible to contemplate /
Brendan Baber and Eric Spitznagel.
p.   cm.
1. Dating (Social customs)—Humor.   2. Courting—Humor.
3. Single men—Humor.   4. Mate selection—Humor.
5. Man-woman relationships—Humor.   I. Spitznagel, Eric.
II. Title.
PN6231.D3B33   1998
818'.5407—DC21   97-24259
CIP

ISBN 978-0-385-48553-1
Copyright © 1998 by Brendan Baber and Eric Spitznagel
All Rights Reserved
Printed in the United States of America
February 1998
146864218
BVG 01

Contents

A Guy's Guide to Dating

Men Are From Mars,
Women Are Out of Their
Freakin' Minds

In the beginning, there was Man. And then Woman came along and everything went straight to hell.

Actually, in the beginning there was probably a lot of primordial sludge that somehow got turned into a one-celled organism, but where's the romance in that? Since those early forms of life reproduced without sex, they don't do a damn thing to help us understand our relationships with women. Intestinal dysentery, maybe, but not the fair sex. So let's toss science out the window and go straight back to mythology.

Like we were saying, it started with Adam, who had a pretty good thing going for a while. He was the star exhibit in Jehovah's personal petting zoo. He grunted and ate wiggly things and spent a lot of time masturbating. Jehovah had the same reaction we'd have to a pet monkey who won't keep his paw off his pud: Get the beast a mate. Okay, so maybe Jehovah should have had Adam "fixed" instead, but hindsight is always twenty/twenty.

Along comes Eve, and she lets this thinly veiled phallic symbol called "the serpent" con her into eating some fruit, and she stops being an animal. Suddenly she has "the knowledge of good and evil." Suddenly she's not a dumb beast anymore. So she figures that misery loves company, asks Adam to have a taste, and he caves in without much protest, which just goes to show that a man's spinelessness in the face of a determined woman is genetic.

Now they aren't even vaguely animals. They're intelligent beings, and they hate it. When Jehovah wants to know whose fault it is, Adam immediately points to Eve, setting up a pattern of blame-shifting that will last for thousands of years. Jehovah doesn't buy the story, and Adam gets evicted from the Garden and is forced to put on clothes and get a real job.

Adam's cohabitation nightmare caused more than just Man's Fall from Grace. He also set the precedent for dating ignorance for centuries to come. Men haven't gotten any smarter over the years, and although we don't have nearly as much to lose as Adam did, our relationships with women still manage to turn into disasters of biblical proportions. But at least Adam had an excuse: He was the first man to attempt dating a woman, so he had no idea what he was getting into. He was bound to screw it up. The rest of us have been at this for a little longer. We should have learned something from history, picked up some granule of knowledge that would have made dating a little easier. But we're still as clueless about women as we ever were, and we show no signs of improving our game. At least we didn't lose our legs, like that serpent.

To be fair, our dating ignorance isn't entirely our fault. Everything we know about women, we've had to pick up on our own. And the majority of it, obviously enough, has been dead wrong. A lot of guys still think that hooting from a car window is the best way to get a woman's attention. And some of us can't imagine talking to a lady without commenting on the size of her mammaries. We just don't understand what women want from us, and no one (especially not women) is willing to give us some much-needed guidance.

Let's face it, men didn't invent the rules of love, women did. In the cosmic scheme of things, men are completely out of the loop. We never got our ID cards and nobody is letting us peek at the instruction manual. We've tried to fake our way through relationships, but by now women know all of our tricks. When we do what we think they want—when we're nice guys who care for their needs and clean up after ourselves—they're suddenly not so interested anymore. If we do the opposite—if we're Don Juan bastards who live dangerously and act like jerks—we still never completely win them over. Sure, they're more likely to fuck us, but eventually we figure out that just because they're fucking us doesn't mean they necessarily *like* us.

We've looked to the so-called dating experts for help, but most of their advice has left us feeling more confused and alienated than we were before. Take, for instance, that feel-good bestseller *Men Are from Mars, Women Are from Venus*. According to the author, John Gray, the key ingredient to a successful relationship is hugs. Lots of hugs. And then, when you're feeling ready for it, more hugs. Snuggling and murmuring "honey-bunny" are optional.

This touchy-feely, soft-as-a-puppy love advice might work for women, but it makes guys want to go screaming for the hills. We're *men,* goddammit, and hugging without fierce back-slapping makes us nervous. Not only don't we relate to this hippy-dippy shit, but the majority of us will not do it. We need a little grime around the edges, a little dirt to go with the flowers which emasculated, self-appointed relationship gurus tell us to sniff. So if all of this unconditional hugging makes you edgy, there's a reason: It's not gonna work.

A woman can be the best thing to happen in your life, or she can ruin it in record time. And let's not get into some statistical duel, where one side says that 45 percent of all men are rapists, and the other side pulls out a chart that shows 79 percent of all women want to castrate Daddy. The real problem—the one that isn't going to go away no matter how hard you hug it—is that 100 percent of all men and women are human. And human beings, as anyone can tell you, are capable of being cowardly, vicious, small-minded, disloyal, un-grateful, putrid, stinking beasts. We defy you to come up with a single act so perverted and horrible that some member-in-good-standing of *Homo sapiens* isn't doing it right now.

As most of you boys know, dating sucks. The reason that dating sucks is that you date human beings.

And this is, we hope, where our book will help. You need prac-tical advice that will get you through a world of broken dreams and used condoms. And rest assured, it *is* possible to have a successful relationship with a woman. But you have to be tricky, and you have to know what to expect. That's what we're here to help you with. We're going to take you on a guided tour through every phase of your love life, from birth to, if you're lucky, marriage. It won't al-ways be easy or pleasant, but if you can manage to suck in your gut and take a few sucker punches, you might make it to the end in one piece.

But probably the best thing we can offer you is a little under-standing. We're on *your* side. Unlike the "experts," who want to spread the blame evenly (since they want everybody to give them money, whether male, female, transgendered, or what-have-you), we're going to take sides. We're guys too, and we understand what a pain in the ass it is to date women. It's us against them, fellas. So let's huddle up and make a game plan. Feel free to spit and cuss with us, and if it makes you feel better, openly mock our female friends. In our world, men may be from Mars, but women are out of their freakin' minds!

Completely unfair, yes, we'll grant you that. Women would probably reverse the equation, and tell us that we're the ones who should be committed. Hmm, come to think of it, they tell us that quite often. So nyah nyah, this is a book for boys, and we're going to stick to our guns. Sure, we may be difficult, lying, unfaithful, and occasionally violent, but women are friggin' *insane*.

Dating Your Mom

(Early Lessons in Love)

For the first couple of years after being born, probably the last thing on your mind is finding a date for Saturday night. Meaningful relationships with the opposite sex just aren't a high priority for the typical toddler, and with good reason. For one, you have enough to worry about already, what with trying to adjust to the strange new environment outside the womb. But the main reason baby boys don't date is because there's not much point to it. Your sexual organs aren't going to become fully functional for at least another ten years, so even if you find the woman of your dreams, there isn't anything you can do about it for a while.

Even though an active love life may be impossible at this time, there's still ample opportunity to exercise your dating chops. While you may be too young to pursue a serious relationship with any of your female peers, there is one special lady who is more than willing to show you how to win the heart of a woman. She is your mentor in love, your girlfriend-by-proxy, your first foray into the wonderful world of romance.

We're talking, of course, about your mom.

We know that sounds creepy, but we're not suggesting that you actually *sleep* with your mom. Like we said before, that's impossible. And even if it wasn't, we'd be the last ones to encourage that kind of behavior. We certainly don't want to be responsible for any Oedipus sex. But your mom *is* a woman, and she is the first woman you'll ever have any kind of relationship with. She's the first woman to feed you, the first to punish you, the first to see you buck-naked, and the first to have unrealistic expectations of you. You may not like to think of her that way, but your mom is, like it or not, your very first girlfriend.

But why should you care? You know how this relationship is going to end before it even begins. There's not much chance that it'll develop into something more serious. And isn't every guy's experience with his mother pretty much the same? Why worry about Mom when there will be other more meaningful (and more fun) relationships in your future?

That is where you're wrong. Your mom is more significant to your love life than any other woman you'll ever know. In fact, she'll have a direct effect on the kinds of women you'll be dating when you become an adult. Long after you've left home and said good-bye to Mommy, your memories of her will be unconsciously determining the women you're attracted to, and repulsed by, for the rest of your life.

Scholars of the mother-son relationship tell us that there are basically two types of guys in the world. Let's call them Boy X and Boy Y. Boy X is looking for a woman who reminds him of Mother. He wants a Virtual Mom, somebody who has all of the traits and characteristics that he loved so much in Mommy. Boy Y would rather have a woman who is the polar opposite of Mom. He *didn't* have a good relationship with his mother, so he'd prefer a mate who doesn't resemble Mommy Dearest in any way.

Which one are you? We can't answer that for you, but we can get you started. Below is a chart of the most common "types" of mommies, along with the kinds of women that a Boy X and Y are likely to be attracted to when they grow up. Keep in mind that these predictions are not necessarily carved in stone. Like any relationship theory, they're only speculative. But if you're like most guys, they can help you make an educated guess of what to expect when you finally join the dating pool.

MOMMY TYPE	BOY X LOOKS FOR . . .	BOY Y LOOKS FOR . . .
Nurturing	A Martha Stewart-esque homemaker who will financially support him and pat him reassuringly on the back during sex.	Multiply-pierced, part-time exotic dancer who steals money from his wallet while he's sleeping.
Super-high expectations that can never be met (a.k.a. the "Show Mom")	An overachieving career woman who will compile dual agendas and demand to know what "improving activities" took place during the day.	A slacker girl who sleeps till noon and quits her job at Starbucks when she realizes that she's being used as a tool of "The Man."
Overprotective	A bossy girlfriend who uses a combination of guilt, cold stares, and brute force to micromanage his life, while also making sure he doesn't achieve too much on his own.	A wide-eyed girl who's looking for Daddy. She hopes to be successful and happy by proxy, pinning all of her dreams on her beloved and oh-so-talented boyfriend.

Religious zealot	A Sunday school assistant who owns a lot of velvet paintings of Jesus and believes that non-procreative sex is an affront to God's will.	A pagan-in-training who attends coven meetings and insists that crystals be arranged around the bed in a pentagram to ward off the wind spirits.
Abusive	A woman who will slap him around when he gets uppity, and generally treat him like dirt.	An obedient girl who cowers in his presence and knows how to take a good spanking.
Divorced and/or working mom (or "Mom? What Mom?")	A woman he can marry, have children with, and then abandon. Child-support checks optional.	A woman with advanced degrees in law and bio-engineering who will give it all up to be a housewife.

The Prepubescent Bachelor's Guide to Kindergarten Babes

Eventually you will have to leave the nest and venture out into the real world. It's your first step toward independence, and more important, your first step toward discovering the galaxy of available girls who are not your mommy.

It's time to meet the gals of kindergarten.

When you first encounter these strange creatures, you'll very likely be baffled by them. "Who are these tiny people who look so different from me?" you'll wonder. "And why can't I look at them without my tongue getting all dry and my heart beating a mile a minute? Am I attracted to them or repulsed by them?" Actually, it's probably a little of both. And not much will change as you learn more about women.

But you're not alone. These girls are just as perplexed by you as you are by them. It's going to take them some time to warm up to you. So don't expect any serious relationships to develop for quite a while. For now, your only job is to get to know your female school-mates and, to the best of your abilities, let them see that you have the potential to be an ideal boyfriend someday.

Here are a few tips to get you started.

1. Say something. If the sexy sweeties at your school are ever going to notice you, you're going to have to swallow your fears and open your trap. Say something, *anything*. The girls will be so surprised that you're actually talking to them that it doesn't matter what you say. Comment on the weather. Complain about your homework. Offer to show them your dead frog collection. This is the only time in your life when having a conversation with a woman is as easy as maintaining eye contact. Enjoy the simplicity while it lasts.

2. Show a little class. It doesn't take much effort to be classy in kindergarten. Most of the other boys in your school are idiots. They've got big melon-shaped heads, a farcical sense of fashion, and alarmingly bad hygiene habits. If you can't be more sophisticated than some snot-faced runt in Spiderman jammies, then you're not really trying. Wash your hair, wear something snazzy, and speak the Queen's English. The girls may not know what to make of you, but they won't be able to take their eyes off you. *Vive la différence!*

3. No kissing. There is absolutely no kissing in kindergarten. If you do, you'll be blacklisted as a pansy by your guy friends and teased within an inch of your life by the girls. Kissing is just too much intimacy for most prepubescents. If you really want to make some kind of physical contact with the sexy mamas at your school, turn it into a game. Spin-the-bottle makes kissing acceptable, and playing doctor is always good for a laugh. If it seems unusual that it's okay to explore a girl's genitals because you're pretending to be a doctor but it's unacceptable to kiss her on the cheek when you're just being yourself, then consider yourself initiated into the paradoxical world of love.

4. Don't push her into the mud and call her a "big ol' dumbie pants." The temptation to physically abuse your female schoolmates can be overwhelming, but resist this urge at all costs. You may think that you're just showing off, but the ladies don't find your bullying tactics attractive in the least. We're not suggesting that you have to be a pussy about it. You don't have to bring them flowers or write poems for them. But if you like a girl, you won't win her affections by pushing her off a swing or calling her "fattie" in front of her friends. If you're trying to be mysteriously aloof, be a little more subtle about it. There's a big difference between playing hard to get and playing *impossible* to get.

5. Don't shit your pants. Nothing says "stay away" like a muffin in the oven. If you can manage to control your bowels for an entire day, the ladies will know you're something special. If you simply have to make Number Two, try to find a bathroom and do your duty in a more suitable locale. The embarrassment of excusing yourself from class for a potty break will be far less humiliating than carrying around an unwanted guest in your pants all day.

6. Take her girlish taunts in stride. There is nothing more terrifying in the world than a gaggle of girls on a teasing spree. If you've been cornered by a young hussy who's discovered that your name rhymes with an embarrassing bodily function and has managed to incorporate in into a clever little song (example: "Bart the Fart/He Likes to Fart," etc.), don't be offended. This is just her way of flirting with you. What she's really trying to say is, "I find you extremely attractive and I'd like to get to know you better."

"This relationship stuff isn't so difficult," you're probably thinking right about now. "I can do this. It's not as impossible as everyone says. I'll be different than the rest. When I grow up, I just know that I'll have a healthy, mature, satisfying love life."

We admire your confidence, but it won't last. In another ten years or so, we guarantee you'll be changing your tune. You'll be as clumsy and inept at relationships as any other man. You may think you're going to be one of the lucky ones, but it won't take long for your delusions of grandeur to crumble.

Where did you go wrong? Why are women avoiding you like the plague? And when you do manage to trick a woman into dating you, why does it always end in disaster? It's not just you, the same thing happens to all men. Despite our best efforts, we just can't figure out how relationships work. We may think we have the skills to win a woman's heart, but eventually we find out that everything we've learned about love as a child was a lie. Someone, or something, has led us astray.

Where did we pick up our dangerous misinformation about women? Was it our parents who lied to us, our childhood friends, our teachers, or maybe late-night cable? If we're young enough, can we blame the Internet?

All of these sources played a role in our faulty education, but none of them had the kind of powerful sway that could make a lasting imprint on us. It had to be something big, something profoundly significant to our lives, something so meaningful and puissant that no young boy could deny its authority. Something like . . .

The *Star Wars* Trilogy

Any guy who came of age in the last thirty years has been influenced by *Star Wars* and its sequels. It was more than just a good sci-fi adventure, it was a blueprint for life. We used the movie as our personal atlas, letting it direct our behavior in all things, especially love. But we didn't take our dating cues from the sugary-sweet Luke Skywalker or the wheezy bad guy Darth Vader. When we wanted to know how to win the heart of a woman, we followed the example of Han Solo.

Who could doubt the dating wisdom of Solo? He was the archetype of the successful stud, the Hugh Hefner of intergalactic relationships, the unrivaled leader of all things *d'amour*. After all, he was the only suitor who managed to win the affections of Princess Leia, the leading lady of all young boys' fantasies. And it didn't hurt that almost every girl in the real world was madly in love with Solo. We saw the posters they hung on their walls, we noticed which action figures they stole from us, and we saw the way they gazed dreamily at him when watching *Star Wars* for the umpteenth time. It didn't take a huge leap of logic to figure out that if we could just be like Solo, we could have any woman we wanted eating out of our hands.

Or so we thought. The sad fact of the matter is, Han Solo was a false god. We studied his every move, thinking that he was giving us all the secrets of what women really wanted from men. But in actuality, he was feeding us a pack of lies that would haunt us for the rest of our lives. Here are just a few of the myths that Harrison Ford and his fictional counterpart passed on to generations of men. *Et tu, Han Solo? Et tu?*

HAN SOLO EXAMPLE	INSIGHT GAINED
He wore the same old smelly outfit in all three movies.	Real men don't have good hygiene.
His best friend was Chewbacca, a big, hairy Wookee.	You should always hang out with guys who are less attractive than you, dumber than you, and, if possible, mute.
He continued to make romantic advances on Princess Leia, despite her repeated refusals and insistence that she didn't like him.	"No" means "yes."
Leia helped him pay off all of his financial debts to Jabba the Hut.	Women are attracted to guys with bad credit.
After saving Leia from the Death Star, he refused to stay with her and join the Rebel Alliance.	Men never commit to a relationship.
His spaceship, the *Millennium Falcon*, was an old, unreliable piece of crap that hardly ever made it to light speed.	A man's "spaceship" is not expected to take a woman to "light speed," if you know what we mean.
He was a consummate smart-ass, constantly mocking Luke, the Rebels, and "The Force."	Guys are expected to make fun of a woman's friends, career choices, and spiritual beliefs.
Leia finally admitted that she loved him after he was captured by the Empire.	Women can't help but fall in love with guys who get into trouble with the law.
Leia risked her life to save him from Jabba's lair.	No matter how badly men screw up their lives, women will always be there to bail them out.
In the end, she picked him over Luke, the clean-cut, responsible man.	Nice guys finish last.

Hand Jive:
The Jerk-Off Years

Even as you were absorbing wrongheaded Leia and Han minutiae, you were probably having your very first sexual experience. You may have stumbled across it by accident, as you sat in the bathtub and discovered that washing your "private parts" was suddenly more fun than it had ever been before. Or maybe one of your friends told you about it and inducted you into the fraternity of self-abuse. Perhaps you happened upon a particularly explicit science textbook that showed you, in shocking detail, just what was so naughty about your naughty bits.

Before long you were addicted to it and hardly a day would go by when you wouldn't lock yourself in the bathroom and enjoy a few "Pictures of Lily." Looking back on it now, it probably seems as if you wasted the majority of your teenage years lost in a haze of masturbatory bliss. And if you're like most guys, you probably feel a little guilty about it. What was the point of all that demented self-stimulation? Couldn't you have spent that time a little better?

Maybe learned a new skill, read a few books, taken up a hobby, *any-thing* more productive?

Well guess what? Masturbation may very well have been the most productive part of your entire teenage experience. What we thought was nothing more than a healthy wank was actually an invaluable education in sex. It taught us everything we will ever need to know for our future sexual relationships with women. If you think about it, there really isn't that much difference between masturbation and sex, except for the obvious addition of a partner. Once we get over the initial thrill of getting an orgasm, we eventually find out that there's more to it than stampeding to the finish line. If we want to truly enjoy masturbation, if we want to reap all of the erotic bounty that it has to offer, if we want to reach that sexual groove that's guaranteed to get the funk out, then we need to adhere to some basic rules of intimacy. And it just so happens that most of these rules are conveniently analogous to sexual encounters of the multiple-partner variety. For example:

- It's always better when you're in the mood. Forced masturbation, like forced sex, is a mundane and soulless activity.

- Self-control is actually a good idea. Premature ejaculation is still a bummer even when you're all by yourself. The clock's not running, guys. You won't be charged for overtime.

- Fantasies can spice up a tired sex drive while also keeping you out of trouble. You may be excited by the idea of sleeping with the pastor's daughter or a sexy German maid, but it'd probably be better for all concerned if you just *imagined* it instead.

• Foreplay is the best way to get your juices flowing. It's easy to get bored with the same old "wham, bam, thank you, Sam" routine. But if you take the time and give some attention to the whole body, you'll be more satisfied in the long run.

• Make sure to lock the doors. You never know who's gonna come barging in unannounced.

But during our prime masturbation years, most of us didn't realize what all that self-abuse was teaching us. We were too busy worrying about whether we were evil people or if we were going to hell. Ah yes, shame and self-loathing: the inoperable cancer of masturbation. It's almost impossible to enjoy liberating solo sex without doing hard time in the prison of guilt. It's been centuries since admitted masturbators were locked up in insane asylums or forced to wear vise-like gadgets on their genitals, but masturbation still hasn't been able to shake its shady and disreputable reputation. Even in this sexually enlightened age, masturbation is still considered to be the worst of taboos. Although every guy does it, very few of us will 'fess up to it. How many times have you heard one of your buddies say, "Yeah, I did myself last night, and boy oh boy, was I *good"?* We're guessing "never," right? Most of us would rather be caught giving oral sex to a pack of horny dwarfs than let anyone know we masturbate.

Part of the problem is that masturbation continues to be shrouded in mystery. None of us know much about it, other than what we've been able to pick up on our own. But the myths are still out there, and many guys still buy into them. We don't have any way of learning otherwise. Dad may have told you about the birds and the bees, but he probably never told you about *just* the bees. School barely taught us about sex—and a Surgeon General got fired for suggesting we be taught about doing it alone—so what hope did we have of picking up any masturbation clues from them? And we certainly didn't learn anything from church, except maybe how our skin will feel when it's being burned to a crisp in the ninth circle of hell. There are a few informative books on masturbation out there, but they're usually written by old hippies whose enthusiastic accounts of circle jerk sessions with young boys tend to leave us feeling a little creeped-out. Where's a guy supposed to find out about the realities of masturbation?

Well, that's what we're here for.

Answers to That Eternal Question, "What Is the Sound of One Hand Clapping?"

1. How much is too much? There is no such thing as "too much" masturbation. Quite frankly, the more you do it, the better it will become. Like any skill, you can only master it after hours and hours of intense practice and study. Think of masturbation as the ultimate endurance test, preparing you for many sexually active years to come. Many guys have bragged that during their potent teen years, they have managed to masturbate up to fifteen times a day. This doesn't seem humanly possible, but if there's any truth to it, we say more power to them. The only time you should even think about stopping is if you begin to develop serious scar tissue or if you notice that you haven't left your room for a few weeks. Frequent masturbation only becomes a detriment when it causes you to ignore basic hygiene and survival needs. If you're masturbating instead of eating, bathing, or experiencing occasional daylight, then you might want to think about laying off the little fella for a while.

2. Will it interfere with my ability to get a real woman?

Let's face it, when you're a teenager, the chances are pretty slim that you're gonna be getting much sex anyway. If you don't masturbate, you're going to endure a lot of annoying and possibly painful erections. Just accept the reality that this is probably the best and only sex that you're gonna get right now and worry about your chances with women later. Besides, in the greater scheme of things, masturbation should just be a side dish, one course from the elaborate menu of sexual dining. To say that sex supersedes masturbation is like suggesting that no one who owns a car occasionally likes to walk instead. You may even discover that sometimes masturbation can be *better* than sex. It does not always take two to tango, but that doesn't mean you've given up dancing partners for life. The only reason to get concerned is if it continues to be your primary source of sexual activity well into adulthood. If you're thirty-five years old, you still haven't had a real sexual experience with a woman, and you've spent your entire life savings on phone sex lines, then it might be time to rethink your situation.

3. What do I need to get started?

Part of the beauty of masturbation is that it is virtually detail-free. All you really need is a comfortable environment, an active imagination, and a lot of free time. If anything needs preplanning, it is the location. The most vital aspect of a pleasant masturbatory experience is finding a spot where you feel safe and without fear that someone, like say your parents, may come barging in at any moment. A lot of guys opt for the bathroom, as this is where they discovered masturbation in the first place and it's not considered unusual to lock the doors and make loud, ecstatic noises. If you feel particularly brave, you might want to move the proceedings to your bedroom, which is a lot more comfortable and, some would say, even romantic. Yes, romance is important, and you'll want to take whatever steps are necessary to get yourself in the mood. Pop a Barry White CD in the boom box, turn down the lights, and whisper sweet nothings into your ear until you're just begging for it. Remember, you are a person, with feelings as real as anybody else, and you don't want to treat yourself like just another piece of meat. Unless you're into rough sex, lubricant is also an important element of masturbation. There are hundreds of everyday household items that can be used for lube purposes, from hand lotion to toothpaste to condiments. But do not, under any circumstances, use soap. Trust us on this one. Soap bad. Soap very bad. Just a dab of soap down under and you won't have any feeling left in your genitals for many, many years to come. And last but not least, keep some cleanup supplies nearby. Don't always assume that there will be some tissue within grabbing distance. You don't want to end up depositing your masculinity on your parents' bath towels or on your favorite t-shirt. Sperm does not come out easily, even after repeated washings. Your only other option is to streak to the nearest tissue dispenser, and with your luck, that's exactly when Grandma will be waking up from her nap. Play it safe and plan ahead.

4. Will it make me go blind or insane? Historically, masturbation has been blamed for every sort of mental and physical malady, from hairy palms to blindness to delinquency to out-and-out insanity. None of it is true, except maybe the insane part. And that is only if you consider staring at scrambled cable porn for hours in a desperate attempt to catch a fleeting glimpse of tit to be insanity. By now most people know that the "masturbation disease" is just a falsehood, but we haven't fully recovered from the stigma that years of masturbation-bashing have left us with. We still have lingering suspicions that masturbation is having a negative effect on our moral fiber, making us bad people who are more likely to commit sexual crimes. If anything, masturbation makes us *less* likely to commit crimes of any sort, sexual or otherwise. It manages to take away all of our sexual frustration and anger and replaces it with giddy satisfaction. A guy who masturbates regularly doesn't have the desire, or energy, to go out and rape someone. Think of it this way: If you masturbate today, the odds are good that you won't be doing hard time in the state penitentiary tomorrow. If you don't do it for yourself, do it for your future.

5. Is it against the word of God? If we are to believe most of today's religious leaders, it most certainly is. But then again, these are the same people who usually end up getting caught in hotel rooms whacking off in front of prostitutes. If they can't follow their own rules, why should we? See you in hell, Mr. Swaggart. There are a few pastors and priests who don't succumb to the nasty habit of masturbation, but that's probably because they're too busy fondling altar boys to bother with solo sex. The Catholic Church might want to think about reversing its stance on masturbation, if for no other reason than that it'd help keep its employees out of trouble. Give them a Saint's Day each week to fantasize about young boys and get it out of their systems. We don't want to assume that we have all the answers, but we're guessing that the Big Guy upstairs will be a little more understanding of bad touching if it applies only to your own person. Speaking of the big G's opinion on the big M, there really isn't any conclusive proof one way or the other that masturbation is a sin. Most religious-minded folk like to point to Onan, who spilled his seed on the ground and pissed off God. But closer scrutiny of this biblical anecdote reveals that Onan was actually engaged in sex with a woman at the time. Coitus interruptus and masturbation don't have much to do with each other, except maybe to people who haven't experienced either. What God is displeased with isn't masturbation at all, just sloppiness. For more details on keeping your seed in check, see our advice on tissue usage above in number three.

6. Will it make my parents hate me? Yeah, probably so. But if they didn't hate you for masturbating, they'd find another reason to hate you. Don't worry about it. They'll get over it eventually.

7. What do I call it? A lot of guys have a problem calling masturbation "masturbation." We have to agree that masturbation is an ugly word, far too utilitarian for an activity filled with so much fun and naughtiness. But there are more ways to describe masturbation than you might expect. After doing extensive research, we discovered thousands of alternative names for masturbation that more accurately embody the frivolity of every guy's favorite hobby. Here are just a few of our favorites:

Adjusting the set, Applying the hand brake, Attacking the one-eyed purple-headed warrior, Auditioning the hand puppet, Backstroke roulette, Bashing the bishop, Basting the roast, Beating the bed flute, Beating the bologna, Beating your meat, Beating off, Beating the old man, Beating the pud, Beef-stroke-it-off, Being your own best friend, Being a virtuoso of the skin flute, Bleeding the lizard, Bleeding the weed, Blowing a load, Blowing your own horn, Bludgeoning the beefsteak, Bopping your bologna, Bopping the Bonzo, Boxing the bald champ, Boxing the Jesuit, Burping the baby, Buttering the corn, Caning the vandal, Charming the snake, Checking for testicular cancer, Choking the cherub, Choking the chicken, Choking Kojak, Choking the sheriff and waiting for the posse to come, Christening the kosher kielbasa, Churning the butter, Cleaning your rifle, Clearing the snorkel, Climbing Mount Baldy, Clobbering the Kleenex, Closet Frisbee, Clubbing the clam, The Colonel Sanders Heimlich Maneuver, Coming to grips with yourself, Coming into your own, Couch hockey for one, Cranking the shank, Crimping the wire, Crowning the king, Crusting the rug, Cuffing the carrot, Dancing with Johnnie One-Eye, Dating Miss Michigan, Dating Rosie Palm and her five sisters, Defrosting the fridge, Den schwanz melken, Diddling, Digging for change, Dipping the deity, Disciplining the monkey, Doing the five-knuckle-shuffle, Doing the pork sword jiggle, Doing the solitary rhumba, Doing the white knuckler, Doing your own thing, Draining the druid, Draining the poisons from the building, Drilling for spooge, Driving the skin bus, Dry-humping the ottoman, Dundering the devil-dolphin, Electing the president, Escorting the one-eyed postal worker out of its denim cell, Faxing Jimmy Dean, Firing the flesh musket, Firing the Surgeon General, Fishing for zipper trout, Flicking the bic, Floating potential down the Nile, Flogging the dog, Flogging your dumber brother, Fly fishing, Freeing Willie, Frosting the pastries, Galloping the antelope, Genitalic stimulation via phallengetic motion, Getting chafed, Getting a date with Slick Mittens, Getting the German soldier marching, Getting the glue stick, Getting a grip on things, Getting off, Getting your palm read by Mr. Softee, Giving it a tug, Giving yourself a low five, Glazing the doughnut, Gluing the lady's good eye shut, Going blind, Going a couple of rounds with ol' Josh, Going on Pee-Wee's little adventure, Grappling the gorilla, Greasing the gears, Greasing the glove, Gripping the pencil, Hacking the hog, Han Solo, Handy work, Hanging Judas till he pukes pennies, Hard labor, Having an arm-wrestle with your one-eyed vessel, Having a conversation with the one-eyed trouser snake, Having a date with Fisty Palmer, Having a one-night-stand with yourself, Having sex with someone you love, Having a tug-of-war with the cyclops, Hitchhiking under the big top, Holding the sausage hostage, Holding your own, Honing your craft, Horny toad waltz, Hugging the hog, Humping the Hindu, Ironing out some wrinkles, Jack hammering, Jacking off, Jazzing yourself, Jerking the gherkin, Jerking Jamby, Jizzlobbing, Juggling the coullions, Justice by your own hands, Kneading the nave, Knuckling the bone, Lathering the limpet, Launching the hand shuttle, Loping the mule, Loves labors lost, Loving the muppet, Lubing the tube, Making the bald man puke, Making Buddha cry, Making friends with Big Ed, Making instant pudding, Making the miter brighter, Making the scene with the magazine, Making yourself at home, Mangling the midget, Manhandling the Monsignor, Manipulating the mango, Manning the cockpit, Manual labor, Master bacon, Milking the cow, Molesting the mole, Mounting a corporal and four, Onan's Olympics, One-gun salute, One-man show, One off the wrist, Orgy of one, Packing your palm, Paddling Pontius Pilate's party pepperoni, Paddling the pud, Painting the ceiling, Pearling the oyster, Peeling some chiles, Performing diagnostics, Petting the puppy, Phoning the czar, Playing a little five-on-one, Playing a one-stringed guitar, Playing peek-a-boo with Mr. Johnson, Playing pocket pool, Playing the skin flute, Playing with the spitting llama, Playing tag with the pink torpedo, Playing Uno, Plucking your twanger, Pole vaulting, Polishing the family jewels, Polishing Percy in your palm, Popping the cork, Popping a nut, Pounding the Preacher, Pounding your pud, Pud wrestling, Pulling the bologna pony, Pulling the cord, Pulling the handbrake, Pulling Peter, Pulling the plow, Pulling the pud, Pulling rank, Pulling your own leg, Pumping the electric goo-gun, Pumping gas at the self-service island, Pumping for oil, Pumping the purple Pontiff, Pumping the stump, Punching the clown, Punching the munchkin, Purging the pentagram, Putting a choke hold on Mr. Clean, Qualifying in the testicular time trial, Raising Lazarus, Raising the mainsail, Ramming the ham, Rapid one arm pull-ups, Reading poetry, Riding the great white knuckler, Rolling your own, Romancing the bone, Romeo and himself, Roping the pony, Roughing up the suspect, Rubbing the pink eraser, Running off a batch by hand, Running the cheetah, Sanding wood, Saying a private prayer in the Church of the First Holy Monkey, Schnauzer Shuffleboard, Scouring the tower of power, Scratching the itch, *Se faire les cinq doigts de la main,* Secret handshake, Self-abuse, Self-inflicted intercourse, The serta solo, Serving the steak, Shaking hands with the master of ceremonies, Shaking hands with the unemployed, Shaking hands with Yul Brynner, Shanking, Sheathin' the Heathen, Shellacking the shillelagh, Shemping the hog, Shifting gears, Shining your helmet, Shooting for the moon, Shooting skeet, Shooting tadpoles at the moon, Shooting your wad, Shucking the corn, Slaking the bacon, Slamming the spam, Slapping the big-nosed Rasta man, Slapping the donkey, Slapping the flesh gopher, Slapping the sloth, Slinging the jelly, Smacking the oompa loompa, Snapping the whip, Solo flight, Spanking Elvis, Spanking the monkey, Speaking in tongues, Spilling the beans, Squeezing the cream out of the flesh twinky, Squeezing the lemon, Squeezing out the toothpaste, Squeezing your cheese-dog, Stinky pinky, Stirring the batter, Stirring the yogurt, Straining the main vein, Strangling the serpent, Stretching the slinky, Striking the pink match, Stroke St. Steven's Slick Slender Salami, Strokin' off, Stroking the one-eyed burping gecko, Stroking the squirmin' German, Summoning the genie, Taking Herman to the circus, Taking matters into your own hands, Taking a nap, Taking the monster for a one-armed ride, Taking ol' one eye through the fly, Taking a shake break, Taking some time off, Talking quietly to yourself, Taming the shrew, Taunting the one-eyed weasel, Tenderizing the meat, Testing your batteries, Throwing up, Tickling the giggle stick, Ticklewigglejigglepickle, Tickling the ivory, Tickling your fancy, Tonking, Torking the fork, Tossing the javelin, Tossing off, Tossing the salad, Tugging the slug, Tugging the tapioca tube, Tuning your instrument, Turning Japanese, Tweaking the twinkle, Twisting your crank, Unloading the gun, Using the Force on Darth Vader, Varnishing the flagpole, Violating the hedgehog, Waking the dead, Waking Wee Willie Wonka, Walking the dog, Walking the plank, Walking the snake, Waltzing with Willy, Wanking with the one-eyed wonder weasel, Waving the magic wand, Waxing your surfboard, Whacking off, Whipping the dummy, Whipping up some sour cream, White-water wristing, Whittling the stick, Windsurfing on Mount Baldy, Wonking your conker, Working out a stiff joint, Wrestling with the bald-headed champion, Wringing out your rope, Wrist aerobics, Yanking the crank, Yanking Spanky, Yanking the Yahoo, Yanking the yo-yo.

High School Confidential

(An Introduction to the
Sixteen-Year-Old Girl)

Sooner or later, you're gonna have to quit your isolated ways and talk to an actual girl. It probably won't be a conscious decision on your part. The urge to meet 'n' greet with the opposite sex will begin to be too powerful to resist. And so you will venture out into the uncharted jungle of high school dating, completely unaware of what lies before you. Be forewarned, it's not all giggles, flirting, and slow-dancing to hard-rock ballads. You'll be facing an obstacle far bigger and more menacing than anything you could have anticipated. To look into its face is to know the meaning of fear. It feeds on the souls of men, leaving nothing but disgrace and destruction in its wake, and laughs at those who dare to beg for mercy. Prepare to experience horror unlike anything you have ever experienced before. Prepare thyself for . . .

the Sixteen-Year-Old Girl!

TIMELINE:

Sixteen-Year-Old Girls Through History

Sixteen-Year-Old Girls are like cats. If they were bigger, they'd eat us. History shows this to be true. Modern-day Sixteen-Year-Old Girls are the descendants of a long line of aggressive, underage harlots. Here are just a few examples.

• **Helen of Troy** According to Homer, the fourteen-year-old Helen of Troy was the most beautiful woman in the world. When Aphrodite, the goddess of love, snatched her out of Sparta and handed her over to the Prince of Troy, it resulted in a ten-year war that left thousands dead. Although Helen may appear to have been an innocent bystander in the whole mess, teenage boys across the world know better. The tradition of guys kicking the snot out of each other to win the hearts of Sixteen-Year-Old Girls continues to this day.

• **Joan of Arc** (1412–31) Considered to be one of the most influential figures in the Hundred

You know the kind we're talking about. They're the young visions of beauty you see every day in high school, with the big doe-like eyes, perfect makeup, poufy hair, and a pure-as-an-angel face. They come in many forms, but by far the most dangerous is the Sixteen-Year-Old Catholic School Girl. The combination of their forbidden status and those sexy plaid-skirt uniforms is enough to give any man with a pulse an erection from forty yards. But a Sixteen-Year-Old Girl can come in all shapes and sizes. She could be a cheerleader, a prom queen, a marching band flutist, your best friend's sister, or even some "mystery girl" who sits behind you in algebra class. They're mostly, but not always, sixteen years old. The Sixteen-Year-Old Girl embodies all girls from high school, from the youngest to the oldest. But the effect that they have on us is always the same.

Although they hardly ever give us a second glance, we are captivated by them. Without even trying, they monopolize our every thought. Once you've been sucked into their tractor beam, there is no chance of escape. Our hands become clammy, our self-esteem drops to zero, and we suddenly understand the lyrics to millions of bad pop songs. We could stare at them for hours, taking in their every move and gesture. We've fantasized about what it would be like to be with them, or even if they just knew our names, and we pray for the day that they finally look our way.

But we can never have the Sixteen-Year-Old Girl. Regardless of how badly we pine for them, despite our spirited attempts to win their affection, they will always reject us. And that is part of the reason we love them so much. They are the Ultimate Unreachables. They are too good for us, too holy to be soiled by mere mortals. We'd probably be disappointed if they did accept us. A Sixteen-Year-Old Girl who says yes loses all of the magic that made her so desirable in the first place. Like Christmas, Sixteen-Year-Old Girls always look better from a distance. They understand this, and that's why they work so hard to keep the illusion alive. In

Years War, Joan of Arc was a peasant who saved the kingdom of France from English domination. When she was only thirteen, she saw a heavenly vision that told her to be a good girl, to obey her mother, and to go to church often. But when she reached seventeen, she decided to blow off the vision and join the war. She inspired a French army to kick some English ass and, more often than not, get themselves killed. She was later burned at the stake, as a warning to Sixteen-Year-Old Girls everywhere to stop messin' with our heads.

• **Juliet** (1595) The saucy ingenue of William Shakespeare's tragedy *Romeo and Juliet,* she is one of the most romantic characters of English literature. But keen scholars of the play realize that Juliet was actually a telling example of the dangerous power that Sixteen-Year-Old Girls possess. Although she put on a show of being loving and devoted, in reality she was a cunning concubine who led Romeo to his almost certain demise. Ol' Willie was teaching us a valuable lesson: Do not trust the intentions of the Sixteen-Year-Old Girl, or she will *destroy you.*

• **Catherine the Great** (1729–96) At sixteen she was married to Grand Duke Peter, the heir to the Russian throne. But Peter was an immature, sickly youth who played with toy soldiers and was widely considered by his countrymen to be "a pussy." Eventually Peter was overthrown and Catherine was declared empress of Russia. The so-called "Catherine gene" continues to thrive in Sixteen-Year-Old Girls to this day, causing them to tolerate unappealing young boys only if they have lots of money or power.

• **Annie Oakley** (1860–1926) During her prime, she was the best-known markswoman in the United States. At the tender age of fifteen, she won a shooting contest with marksman Frank Butler and was invited to join Buffalo Bill's Wild West Show. If "Little Sure Shot" proved anything, it was that men love Sixteen-Year-Old Girls who are skilled with firearms. But deep in our hearts, we are also scared shitless by them. As Mr. Butler could testify, Sixteen-Year-Old Girls learn to use guns for one reason: to shoot *guys!*

• **Lolita** (1955) The anti-heroine of Vladimir Nabokov's

a way, it's very much a predetermined agreement. We want you but you won't let us have you. We can all agree on the simple beauty of the unattainable romance. And so the dance continues.

But just because it's impossible doesn't mean that we won't try. In true underdog tradition, we're determined to hit them with everything we've got and see if we can't break through their barriers of steel. Guy mythology tells us that a few lucky souls have actually managed to win the heart of a Sixteen-Year-Old Girl. Although we're dubious of these claims, it gives us enough confidence to at least try our luck and play the odds. And that's all that really matters anyway. When courting the Sixteen-Year-Old Girl, it's the journey that counts, not the destination. It's an opportunity to test our seduction skills in the most difficult arena, to strut our stuff in the Olympics of Dating. As far as women go, it'll never be this difficult again. If you can manage to connive even one iota of affection from a Sixteen-Year-

Old Girl, the rest of your dating life will seem like child's play by comparison.

On the flip side, if we never dare to enter the Sixteen-Year-Old Girl's Labyrinth of Love Denied, it will surely haunt us forever. Better to have loved and been publicly humiliated in front of all of your friends then never to have loved at all. Or something like that. Trust us, as bad as it sounds, you'll end up paying more dearly tomorrow for the missed opportunities you let slip by today.

To assist you in the hopeless quest of attracting a Sixteen-Year-Old Girl, we've done most of the homework for you. After carefully studying the mating patterns of these slippery creatures, and talking to teenage boys from past and present, we've created a cheat sheet that may well prove to be invaluable to you. Study it well, and prepare yourself for the Heart of Darkness.

God save your soul.

novel, Lolita was a twelve-year-old girl who was seduced and kidnapped by a middle-aged geezer named Humbert Humbert. But Lolita was by no means a victim. This sexy nymphet encouraged Humbert's obsession, although their affair was destined to self-destruct. The story is a poignant warning to all young boys: You will never escape the siren song of the Sixteen-Year-Old Girl. If you're not careful, you could end up like Woody Allen, Jerry Lee Lewis, or Joey "Baby, I'm a Star" Buttafuoco. Do not confuse *Lolita* with a love story, or you'll eventually find yourself in deep doo-doo.

• **Brooke Shields** (1980) The sultry fifteen-year-old model appeared in a TV ad for Calvin Klein jeans that shocked and aroused a nation of young boys. Squeezing her body into a pair of skintight jeans, Shields posed the rhetorical question: "You know what comes between me and my Calvins? Nothing." An admitted virgin, the overtly sexual swaggering of Shields was a blatant act of violence. Sure, she's sexy, *but you can't have her!* Nobody can have her. But you're welcome, even encouraged, to take a long, lingering look at her body. What was she trying to do, kill us?

• **Alicia Silverstone** (Early '90s) The sixteen-year-old blond bombshell was the leading lady of a trilogy of Aerosmith rock videos. She was a bungee-jumping runaway in "Cryin'," a fantasy cyberbabe in "Amazing," and a skinny-dipping, older-man-teasing lust-monger in "Crazy." Although not necessarily dangerous, she did confirm our suspicions that Sixteen-Year-Old Girls are actually having a lot more fun than we are.

• **Brenda from *Beverly Hills, 90210*** (1990–94) The *coup de bitch* of the popular high school drama, Brenda was a man-hating, heartbreaking, jaw-smashing Über-Vixen who was impossible to resist. She didn't just break up with a guy, she made damn sure he was left with enough pain and humiliation to last him well into adulthood. We've all known Sixteen-Year-Old Girls like Brenda, and we've all secretly lusted after them. They present a challenge greater than climbing K2. But at least with mountain climbing we stand a chance of survival.

• **The Gore Girls** (1992–present) The three teenage girls who entered the White House and our hearts in 1992 have

Today Her Training Bra, Tomorrow the World!

1. Sports jerseys

In the food chain of high school, the football players are always on top. Sixteen-Year-Old Girls know this, and that is why they are invariably drawn to them. But don't be mistaken: The Sixteen-Year-Old Girl does not like the football jock any more than the rest of us. What she really wants from him is his jersey, that skin-like trophy that proves she is a member of the popular crowd. If you're not already on your school football team, join it *now.* It doesn't matter if you actually play, or even if you show up for games. All you need is that precious jersey, which will have Sixteen-Year-Old Girls lining up outside your door to get a taste of the precious cloth. Handing over your jersey brings with it some fringe bene-firs that mortal men can only dream of. She'll allow you to hold her hand, to kiss her, and, in rare cases, even to cop a quick feel. But don't get all excited. Remember that her affection is mostly for show, and the odds are slim that she will want to be with you when her friends are not around to witness it. But what the hell, you'll take what you can get, right?

2. Cute guys from TV and the movies From Scott Baio to Matthew Perry, Sixteen-Year-Old Girls crave the male cuties who are actually out of *their*

hypnotized us all, and they know it. Sarah, Kristin, and Karenna are almost too good to be true—sexy as movie stars and spitting distance from massive political power. Better yet, they've shown that they can be both naughty *and* nice. The twelve-year-old Karenna played Prince's pop ditty "Darling Nikki" for her mommy, Tipper, who promptly led a crusade to stamp out all obscene rock lyrics. And then in 1995, sixteen-year-old Sarah was caught partying with beer in a car. They are truly the Yin and Yang of Sixteen-Year-Old Girls, embodying the best of all possible worlds.

reach. Once you figure out what kinds of stud-muffins get her heart beating fast, you'll become better equipped to engage her in meaningful conversation. Read plenty of teeny-bopper magazines, such as *Tiger Beat* and *Sassy,* and learn the latest trends in cute-guy show business. Find out which TV shows and movies have the highest quotients of cute guys and watch them regularly. And then when the opportunity arises, discuss what you have learned with her. She'll be mighty impressed if you can identify any of the cutie-pies from *Friends,* and flabbergasted if you seem to know more about them than she does. But don't get carried away. Teen-star worship is dangerous terrain, especially for guys. If you seem too interested, she'll eventually get the idea that you're some kind of girlie-man. Show just enough enthusiasm to convince her that you do indeed care about her needs. Anything more than that will thrust you into "limp-wrist" territory.

3. Ponies Most Sixteen-Year-Old Girls developed a passion for ponies as prepubescents, and have yet to get over the horrifying realization that they will never actually own one of these foul beasts. Anybody who has seen the inner sanctum of a Sixteen-Year-Old Girl's room could tell you that they have an obsession with ponies that borders on religion. If it isn't ponies, it's unicorns, but the symptoms are the same. Their walls are covered with posters of these hoofed creatures, and almost everything they own—from clothing to notebooks to "feminine products"—has a picture of a happy-looking pony on it. Although you may find the temptation to mock their pony-love overwhelming, you should never *ever* make your true feelings known. If you do so, you will be blacklisted and forced to endure your remaining high school years in solitude. If she shows you any of her prized pony or unicorn collectibles, smile like a good boy and say, "Ooooh, that's pretty."

4. Music videos Do not second-guess the seductive powers of music videos. All those long-haired freaks in leather hip-huggers may look absurd to us, but for the Sixteen-Year-Old Girl it can be an aphrodisiac of awesome power. When she says, "I want my MTV," she's not kidding around. But keep in mind that it's not always obvious what kinds of videos will make a Sixteen-Year-Old Girl all hot and bothered. It's a delicate balance of imagery and music that can't possibly be predicted. She might need the raw power of speed-metal to get her going, or maybe the soft-as-a-bunny Paul Simon is enough to make her purr. In any case, there's not much you can do to control what she sees anyway. You're at the mercy of the programmers who decide what videos will air. The best you can do is try to get her to watch TV with you long enough for the "Chosen Video" to make its appearance. If you're lucky, you'll strike gold eventually.

5. Passing notes in class The Sixteen-Year-Old Girl has a particular distaste for school, so she'll gladly accept any distraction that will take her attention away from the mundane routine of learning. Regardless of who you are, she'll be happy to receive a note from you either during or between classes. Odds are she will return the favor, and before long you will have established an actual rapport with her. Don't jump to the conclusion that this is the beginning of a relationship. Note-passing is a recreational sport that doesn't always result in intimacy. If you want to find out just how serious her intentions are, look for telltale indicators in her notes. If she decorates them with hearts, flowers, and smiley faces, and signs her name with the noncommittal "Luv," then she is probably sending you subtle clues that your note-passing relationship is ready to progress to the next level. Always practice caution in composing your note content. You never know who else might be reading it, or when it's going to be snatched away by an angry teacher. Sixteen-Year-Old Girls have a low tolerance for embarrassment, and a single public reading of your note could be enough to cause her to 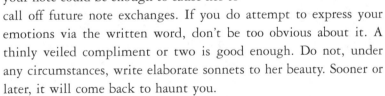 call off future note exchanges. If you do attempt to express your emotions via the written word, don't be too obvious about it. A thinly veiled compliment or two is good enough. Do not, under any circumstances, write elaborate sonnets to her beauty. Sooner or later, it will come back to haunt you.

6. Facial Hair Sixteen-Year-Old Girls love older men, and nothing indicates advanced age better than a little facial hair. But beware, not every guy looks good in facial hair. More often than not, a mustache or beard on a teenage boy only confirms his geekiness.

This is especially true if you aren't able to grow enough facial hair to make it noticeable. There is nothing more ridiculous than a microscopic mustache that looks more like a nose shadow than actual stubble. Before you decide to let your whiskers grow unchecked, take a moment for honest evaluation. How often is it *necessary* for you to shave? If you don't take razor-to-face more than once a month, then it's probably unlikely that you have what it takes to grow some bona fide facial hair.

7. Finding "our" song If you're one of the lucky few who've somehow managed to dupe a Sixteen-Year-Old Girl into dating you, then you'll want to give some serious thought into picking a pop-rock ballad to represent your relationship. The relationship song (otherwise known as "our" song) is akin to the wedding ring for married couples: It is tangible evidence of your love for each other. Sure, *you* know it's bullshit, but the wise boyfriend will feign enthusiasm for this hollow tradition. But you don't just pick a relationship song and forget about it. It is an invaluable commodity that will play an active role in the rest of your high school dating life. It's the song you'll slow-dance to at the prom. You quote lyrics from it during intimate exchanges. You'll call up local radio stations and request that it be played as a "special dedication." And, of course, you'll say "Listen, honey, they're playing 'our' song" every time you hear it. Relationship songs must be decided on together, but any Sixteen-Year-Old Girl will probably expect you to bring some of your own ideas to the table. This doesn't mean that you have to listen to every Top 40 hit ever recorded. Relationship songs are easy to identify, as long as you know what to look for. To qualify for "our" song status, it must adhere to at least one of the following rules:

- It includes the lyrics "I will always love you," or a similar mention of eternal affection.

- The lead singer is a cutie-pie. (See number two above for more details.)

- The music is not overly complicated or "funky." If it contains more than three chords, it's too confusing to hum along with.

8. Cars It's no secret that Sixteen-Year-Old Girls are drawn to guys with cars, particularly if they don't have a car of their own. After all, no dignified Sixteen-Year-Old Girl would be caught dead taking the bus to school. But all cars are not created equal. A car is more than just a set of wheels, it also reflects your personality and, as a result, what kinds of Sixteen-Year-Old Girls you'll attract with it. Before you choose an automobile that may very well determine the fate of your high school love life, take a moment to familiarize yourself with the credentials of some of the most popular teenage-guy cars.

TYPE OF CAR	WILL SHE LIKE IT?
Sports car	It can't be denied that the babes will always go gaga for a sleek-looking sports car. If it goes fast and makes a lot of cool engine sounds, the girls will want to ride in it. But despite all the frills, it does have a deadly Achilles' heel that can backfire on you. Many sports cars tend to be too small, with limited room up front and often no backseat whatsoever. Making out in one of these damn things can be an impossible endeavor.
Dad's car	Regardless of how cool the car may be on its own, if your dad owns it, she's gonna think you're a dork. Some guys have tried lying, but sooner or later they're gonna find out. Nothing ruins a date quicker than having to get the car home early because Daddy wants to use it. Driving your dad's car says one thing to a girl: This guy is *cash poor.*
Jeep	Your chances are fifty-fifty that she will. Some girls find them obnoxious and extremely uncomfortable (and the open roof will mess up her hair). But others think they're downright rugged and sexy. If she's a sporty gal who loves the outdoors and taking a ride through some rough terrain, you'll have it made.

Volkswagen van	You're definitely going to be attracting the pot-smoking, Horde Fest–following, friendship-bracelet-making set with this one. If that's your intention, you can't go wrong. But if you're looking to woo girls of a slightly higher social status, you're wasting your time.
An early eighties beater	It depends. If you let the car rot, then probably not. But if you fix it up a little—add some tacky seat covers, a bitchin' stereo system, and maybe some oversized fluffy dice—then you've got something that'll turn her head. Ladies love the pimpmobile!

9. Dry-Humping You know what we're talking about. It's the "First Base of Love," the closest most teenage guys ever get to actual sex. Although few of us have performed the dry-hump with the Sixteen-Year-Old Girl of our choice, sooner or later we all get to experience it at least once. The dry-hump is basically sex in clothes. There's no nudity involved, much less penetration, but it can be profoundly satisfying nonetheless. Now more than ever, it really is the "motion of the ocean" that counts, so be prepared to bump and grind with everything you've got. If you're good, you may even give her an orgasm, which is no small task. Anyone who has ever tried to find a clitoris through a tight pair of acid-washed jeans knows exactly what we're talking about. If you haven't gotten any dry-humping from your main squeeze yet, just be patient and follow her lead. Guys are hardly ever expected to initiate the dry-hump. She'll get around to it when she's good and ready. After all, it's not a question of whether or not you're horny. Everybody in the world knows that *you're* horny. But the ladies take a little longer to get warmed up and they may need to become more comfortable with you before they're ready to let you feel up the goodies. If you're having a hard time waiting, go back to the masturbation section and read it again.

Higher Learning

(Or, How to Spend $15,000 a Year to Get Stoned, Date Lesbians, Argue with Feminists, and Contract Herpes)

If you're like most guys, you probably think that it's a good idea to go to college. You've been conned into believing that it's vital to your future and may even teach you something valuable and worthwhile. But once you get there, you'll discover that college really isn't that much different from high school. There are ornery, underpaid teachers, mind-numbingly boring class curricula, drunken, inattentive students, and a rigid social structure that, once again, exists only to exclude you.

But this is not to suggest that college is a complete waste of time. Even with all of its faults, college does possess one key element that almost makes it worth the expense. No, it has nothing to do with expanding your intellectual horizons or any other bullshit claim that universities will try to sell you on in their glossy and grossly inaccurate brochures. The truth is, the only good thing that college has to offer is . . .

Casual Sex

If you were born during the last decade, you're probably unfamiliar with the concept of casual sex. You may have heard rumors about it, but like any right-thinking guy you assumed that it was just a cultural myth, like Santa Claus or Reaganomics. But believe it or not, casual sex is a reality. Here are a few rudimentary definitions of what constitutes casual sex:

cas•u•al sex (kazh'*oo*-uhl seks), n. *{LL. casualis secare (L. causus, sexus)}*

> *1. an impersonal, anonymous union between two horny adults;*
> *2. an integral ingredient of the Sexual Revolution, a counterculture movement of the sixties and early seventies;*
> *3. a very bad 1988 movie starring Lea Thompson and Victoria Jackson.*

For the purposes of our discussion, we will ignore definition number three. The casual sex that interests us is the physical act described in the first definition. This strange phenomenon occurs when two people, often complete strangers, agree to have sex with each other for no other reason than experiencing an orgasm, or "getting off." After the sex is over, they usually go their separate ways and never see each other again. There are none of the entanglements that usually accompany most sexual encounters. There is no phone call the next day, no guarantees of future rendezvous, no "being sensitive to her needs," and, in many cases, not even cab fare home. It is the ultimate in low-maintenance intimacy.

Casual sex first came into vogue in the sixties, thanks to things like the pill and rock and roll music. Many people discovered their sexual organ for the first time and, like kids with a new toy, they wouldn't stop playing with it. These pioneers of casual sex, or "hippies" as they often called themselves, believed that having sex with strangers was an important step toward achieving personal freedom. It was a means for them to reject the values and morals of their parents, and to defy the order of the Establishment. Or something like that. Nobody seems to know for certain why all that sex was taking place. But one thing was for certain: It was unbelievably easy to get laid. A typical date looked something like this:

GUY: Hey, baby.
GIRL: Hey, Daddy-O. What's cooking?
GUY: Just peace and love, baby. You wanna fuck?
GIRL: That sounds groovy to me.
GUY: Right on, baby.

A lot of old people have very fond memories of the sixties, and they like to believe that it was an exciting, highly creative period in American history. They insist that there was a lot more to the sixties than just casual sex. And there is some truth to this. The hippies of the sixties also enjoyed things like overdosing on drugs, living in mini-vans, getting beaten with nightsticks at political conventions, dancing around in mud, and bad hygiene. But the truth of the matter is, the only reason that anybody remembers the sixties is that there was a lot of really good fucking going on.

But then the eighties came along and ruined everybody's fun. Casual sex all but disappeared in the decade of yuppies and parachute pants. It may have been because all the hippies were finally settling down and getting real jobs, which left them with no free time for things like casual sex. It may have been because the government had secretly employed a team of scientists to invent new and more deadly sexual diseases like AIDS. Whatever the reason, nobody seemed to be enjoying much casual sex anymore.

Nobody, that is, except for college students. After all, college students *invented* casual sex, and they weren't about to give it up just because the rest of the world had decided to go pro-monogamy. Oh sure, occasionally there are excited reports from the media that casual sex isn't as prevalent on college campuses as it used to be. Every year the American Council on Education sponsors a high-profile survey of college freshmen from across the country, and every year they announce that "College freshmen are voicing dwindling support for casual sex." According to the ACE survey, the percentage of college students who condone casual sex has been dropping steadily since the eighties, and in 1996 it reached an all-time low of around 43 percent.

"Well, how do you explain that?" you may be asking. "If you think casual sex is still popular on college campuses, how do you account for the ACE's carefully gathered data that seems to directly contradict you?"

We'll tell you how we can explain it. The students who were surveyed were lying. That's right, *lying.* Don't look so surprised, you know it's true. College students are trained to be professional liars. They get into college by lying, and they manage to fake their way through four years of scholastic bullshit by lying. Lying is expected of them. A college student will only tell you what he or she thinks you want to hear, especially if you seem to be in a position of authority. They respect the notion of conventional wisdom. Even if they know it's a crock, they'll still agree with it if they think that doing so will get them a passing grade.

But you're still not convinced. "I'm still not convinced," you say. "It's your word against theirs, and they have all kinds of fancy numbers and percentages to back them up. What do you have?" Well, if it's percentages you're looking for, we have plenty of that. We understand how this game is played. We know that you're far more likely to go along with our crazy theories if we have some official-sounding statistics to make it sound more, well, *official.* So that's exactly what we've done. We visited a few college campuses and talked to students about their opinions on casual sex. Sure, it's very likely that they just lied to us too. But as long as we got the data we came looking for, we don't much care one way or the other. And besides, we got to ask a bunch of kids all sorts of personal and embarrassing questions about their sex life.

How often do you engage in casual sex?
    80%—All the time
    15%—Once in a while
    5%—With any luck, tonight

How would you define "Safe Sex"?
    7%—Abstinence
    8%—Using a condom
    85%—Not calling your partner the next day

How much of this casual sex would you define as being particularly "kinky"?
    47%—Most of it
    35%—Some of it
    18%—How do you mean "kinky"?

Well, do you use vibrators, nipple clamps, handcuffs, or other sexual toys with your casual sex partners?
    23%—You betcha!
    31%—Only if I'm really, really drunk
    46%—None of your damn business

Do you have any color photographs of your casual sex encounters that you'd be willing to share with us? Solely for research purposes, of course.

33%—I'm sorry, *what?*

42%—What are you, some kind of pervert?

25%—Sure. Check out my web page.

Would you be willing to have casual sex with the authors of this book?

75%—No

20%—Maybe

5%—Only if the book is a bestseller

But what if you were really, really drunk?

52%—No

45%—Undecided

3%—Get away from me or I'm going to call campus security

As the results of our survey reveal, there is definitely lots of casual sex taking place in college. And not only that, there's also plenty of nasty, perverted, downright lewd sex going on. Quite frankly, we're more than a little envious. The sex wasn't this good when *we* went to college. What in God's name are they teaching college kids these days?

"Wow, that sounds great," you're probably saying. "You've convinced me. I want to go to college too so I can get me some of that super-cool casual sex. What do I need to do to get started?" Actually, not much at all. Just follow our simple two-step formula and you'll be well on your way to enjoying everything that college life has to offer:

1. *Enroll in a college.*
2. *Find a college woman willing to have casual sex with you.*

The Five Basic Types of College Women

TYPE	ADVANTAGES	DRAWBACKS	PREFERENCE IN A MATE
Intellectual	Quiet, will help you do your homework, lots of free computer equipment, low expectations in a mate, interesting conversations, pent-up sexuality	Nerdy, no friends, makes you feel like an idiot, unisex clothes, wants to spend Friday night studying, knows all the lines to every Monty Python skit and will recite them to you.	Professor
Sorority sister	Predictable, lots of free alcohol, if you strike out with one there's plenty more just like her, lesbian overtones, looks and acts like a Sixteen-Year-Old Girl	Prone to fits of giggling, monosyllabic, Republican fathers, a magnet for date rape, looks and acts like a Sixteen-Year-Old Girl	Fraternity brothers
Jockette	Nice body, aerobic sex, thighs that could snap your neck, cares less about academia than you do, will actually watch the Super Bowl with you	Dumb as dirt, sweats a lot, majority of dates involve weight-lifting, stronger than you, calls you "little man," hairy upper lip	Michael Jordan

Art major	Sexually promiscuous, no bras, lots of free drugs, too self-obsessed to notice your faults, sleeps late, amicable disposition, undeniably hip	Delusions of grandeur, unreliable, spacey, bad hygiene, will read her poetry aloud, no future prospects	A poet and/or rock guitarist
Feminist	Easy to make fun of	Whining, no sense of humor, hairy armpits, doesn't like you, probably won't have sex with you, convinced that you're a rapist	Jockette

A Few More Thoughts on Feminists

Okay, we'll admit that there's a little more to feminists than the one-dimensional stereotype mentioned above. Although your gut impulse may be to mock them, it's a good idea to become more familiar with what feminism is really all about, since the odds are high that you're going to run into a fair amount of it during your stay in college. It may be in the form of a leaflet, a "take back the night" march, a public speech, or a girlfriend who believes that body hair removal is a symbol of patriarchal oppression.

No doubt the whole thing will leave
you with strange and contradictory feelings.

Sure, equal rights for everyone seems like a
great goal, but how do you accommodate a
philosophy, such as feminism, that doesn't
make room for you? How can you co-habit
with a worldview that can, at times, attack you by
virtue of what you *are?* The whole thing is terribly
confusing. Let's back up and take a slow, careful look at it from a guy's perspective:

On one hand, giving women a fair shake
seems like a damn good idea. On the other, people who say that men are the root of all evil and
women the font of all virtue are delusional. People are, after all, just people. And it doesn't matter
whether a person is male or female if s/he is a jealous, squinty-eyed,
untrustworthy little shit. When you know someone who's an evil
human being, neither a penis nor a vagina seems like a good excuse.

But your relationship with feminism is going to be both less and
more complicated than you suspect. When you've struggled to decide whether or not you are a feminist man, or a sort-of-feminist
man, or maybe even an antifeminist man, you've been playing a
sucker's game, where the prize is even less appealing than the orange
stuffed animal you get to lug around the amusement park after you
lob three bean bags in the plastic clown's mouth. Why, you ask?

There is no such thing as feminism.

Oh, there *was* at one point, have no doubt, but by now it's more
of an excuse to get print and radio coverage. You laugh? You say we
lie? Think again.

Some feminists claim that women should be equal to men; others
declare that they should be superior. Some argue that women have
always been better than men, and it's just time to make it more bla-

tant; others suggest that "traditional family values" (whatever the hell those are) should rule, and women should reincorporate babies and fishnet stockings into their lives. Looking at the vast sea of contradictory statements, we should accept what has been true for almost a decade: Feminism is whatever the woman you're speaking to at the moment says it is. Don't argue, don't protest, don't get dragged into a lose-lose sucker scenario. There is no coherent body of thought that can be called feminism.

Stoicism was a *real* philosophy: It said you should stay cool whether the world treated you nicely or horribly. Democracy has a philosophy: Everybody should have some say in government, usually by means of voting for people they don't know or like. Even communism has a unified ideology that stands up to logic, if not reality. But feminism is an umbrella term that covers about six hundred separate bodies of thought. Lumping Nancy Friday and Andrea Dworkin into the same philosophical group is, well, remarkably stupid. It's exactly this sort of fuzzy logic that allowed noted liar and fat sissy Rush Limbaugh to use the term "feminazis," since he could cull the most extreme examples of feminist thought and apply it to the splintered whole. But it's a safe bet that the "feminism" that Rush denounced and the feminism that Susie Bright practices are two animals which have evolved to the point where they either can't mate at all, or their offspring would be twisted and sterile.

To provide a brief example, we called up four women of varying ages and asked each one what feminism means to them. It's an unscientific sort of poll, but it illustrates our point nicely.

Woman 1 (age 38): "{Feminism} is about economic and social equality, nothing more or less."

Woman 2 (age 26): "When you can wear high heels and men's cologne at the same time, that's feminism."

Woman 3 (age 19): "It shows that most men are potential date rapists, and women have been suckered into doing their bidding. The women who don't get this are under the spell of their no-necked, jock-assed, fraternity boyfriends."

Woman 4 (age 11): "It's about being feminine, the way a girl would be. Wearing dresses and flirting and stuff."

There was a time, long ago, when feminism was a straightforward proposition, and everybody agreed that it stood for equal rights and equal obligations before the law. Essentially what Woman 1 said up above and Susan B. Anthony said a century before her. This meant easy-to-understand things like the right to vote, the right to work, and the right to get killed by strangers while serving in the armed forces. You know, all of that life-liberty-pursuit-of-happiness stuff we get misty-eyed about whenever people get run over by tanks while protesting for it someplace else.

But the most basic goals were achieved here in the United States, and it happened a while ago. As the issues of gender rights have gotten more subtle, women have splintered up into a myriad of subgroups and tangential beliefs. But don't think for a moment that this is a "woman thing" exclusively, since the tendency to wander off and do your own thing when there isn't an obvious goal is a fact of the human condition. Just think about the last time you and your friends tried to decide what to do on Friday night. Enough said.

So how the hell do you handle this? For instance, if you're out for dinner with your favorite lady friend, do you split the check evenly, since you're both empowered, actualized individuals? Or do you pick up the tab, to demonstrate the fact that, despite changes in sexual relations, you still believe in chivalric gestures?

As nice as it would be if there were some standard answer for this predicament, you're going to have to play it by ear. Remember, *feminism is whatever the woman you're speaking to says it is.* So follow her lead and listen to her closely. If she makes frequent references to Patricia Ireland, shows you a signed copy of *Backlash,* and suggests that all heterosexual intercourse is violation, split the check evenly and tell her that you're a bisexual who likes to be taken forcibly by Mexican men, but you're willing to experiment with women from time to time. If, instead, she talks at length about Camille Paglia, shows you her dog-eared copy of *Tropic of Cancer,* and steers the conversation toward bondage etiquette, pay the check in cash, leaving the waiter a 30 percent tip.

But whatever you do, don't let yourself get dragged into an argument about the politics of men and women. We aren't sure who decided that the private conduct of romance and dating should be politicized, but it was a rotten idea to the core, and somebody should be issuing a public apology right about . . . now.

Life is complex, contradictory, and full of surprises. It's always been that way, and it always will. Anyone who hopes to understand a human endeavor such as dating must appreciate the subtleties and accept the paradoxes.

Politics, on the other hand, is about reducing life to a simple slogan or idea that will motivate a lot of people. That's why political art tends to be boring and preachy. And that's why politics and dating make horrible bedfellows. While we're on the subject, that's why feminist theater sucks. (And just so you know we aren't picking on the ladies, we'll point out that socialist theater, fascist theater, and postmodern theater all suck, too.)

If you're trying to make it work with a woman who brings her politics to bed, it's probably best to find someone who uses more interesting things between the sheets. Like, say, handcuffs or a multi-attachment vibrator.

Once you've figured out what kind of woman you want to be with (and we can only hope that we've convinced you to stay away from women who bring politics to bed), the next stage in your quest for casual sex is to find a way to convince her to have sex with *you*. Although there are many ways to do this, the solution that most every guy will invariably turn to is . . .

Drugs, the College Man's Best Friend

There is no better way to enjoy the fruits of casual sex than by embracing the mystical power of drugs. And there's a very good reason for this. When we're sober, we realize just how stupid it is to have sex with a complete stranger. But thanks to drugs, we're able to do away with things like common sense and good judgment. It gives us the confidence we need to get naked with just about anybody. We don't need to know them. Hell, we don't even need to *like* them. They could be a one-eyed bag lady with droopy breasts, blistering canker sores, and breath that smells like a dog. Drugs help us realize that anything with a hole is a prime candidate for a night of thigh-slapping bliss.

You shouldn't have any problem finding drugs at your college. Most colleges are basically just huge pharmacies, with more drugs for sale than class textbooks. The only challenge you may encounter is the staggering array of drugs to choose from. There are so many options that the novice druggie may not have any idea where to begin. Which drugs are most likely to have the libidinal effects that you're looking for? And which drugs will make you and your partner do things that you both may regret in the morning? Choosing the right drug for you can make the difference between a night of pleasant casual sex and a night of uncontrollable vomiting.

TYPE OF DRUG	EFFECTIVENESS	SIDE EFFECTS
Beer	A popular favorite on college campuses everywhere, it is believed to be the perfect aphrodisiac. But in all honesty, it has a rather negligible effect on seduction. College students get drunk because they want to get laid, and beer creates the illusion that they're out of control. In most cases, beer serves as little more than an advertisement for sex, not a means to an end.	You'll both be left with the haunting sensation that if you weren't sleeping with each other, you'd be sleeping with the next available warm body.
Hard liquor	Although hard liquor has a (much deserved) bad reputation, it is guaranteed to put both you and your partner in the lovin' mood toot sweet. A little bourbon or tequila is all it takes to ensure a night of sloppy sex.	You may not like what you turn into. There's something about hard liquor that makes men *and* women turn into jerks. You'll spit and curse, get into arm-wrestling competitions, and try to start bar brawls. Is the easy sex really worth watching an otherwise beautiful woman mutate into a truck driver?

Pot	Although it threatens to become as big a college cliché as beer, pot does have some real effects on your libido. That is, of course, if you and your honey can manage to stop giggling.	If she gets a bad case of the munchies, she could become more aroused by a bowl of Cap'n Crunch than anything you have to offer.
LSD	Lock the door, take out the lava lamp, put on a little Blues Traveler, and let Lucy do the rest. If she feels safe and "digs your vibe," then you're guaranteed a little cosmic nookie.	A wide array of scary hallucinations. If you see her face melting, you may be too freaked out to enjoy sex. And if she looks at your penis and sees a gargoyle, or worse yet, her *dad,* you can forget about getting any sexual healing.
Misc. (coke, crack, heroin, poppers, etc.)	If all else fails, dipping into the "grab bag" of drug possibilities might be just the jump-start your sex life needs. Pharmaceuticals can be dangerous, but they can also turn tired genitals into all-night party machines.	Many of these drugs can have such an orgasmic effect that they make sex seem almost redundant and therefore unnecessary.

The Truth About Fraternities (Or, Girls Doff Their Sweaters for Guys with Greek Letters!)

One of the most enduring myths about casual sex in college is that most of it happens in or near fraternity houses. For those of you not familiar with these antiquated institutions, fraternity houses are places where college men go to drink beer, abuse each other for fun, and, supposedly, get a lot of free sex. This myth has only been reinforced by movies like *Animal House,* which tried to make us believe that fraternities were made up of lovable losers who didn't like studying but sure knew how to party. And women would flock to them, practically begging to have their panties ripped off and be ravaged by fat pigs like John Belushi. With this kind of reputation, who *wouldn't* want to join a fraternity?

But we were dubious, so we decided to find out for ourselves just how much sex and sin were taking place in a real fraternity house. We visited a college fraternity on a Saturday night, for a party that was advertised as "The Most Rocking Event of the Semester!" The fraternity members, or "brothers," promised us that it would be a festivity of Dionysian proportions. There would be plenty of women, they said, and every one of them would be a horny fuckbeast on the hunt for some "Greek Groin." Needless to say, we were enthused by the prospect, and we even went so far as to purchase a few Greek letter sweatshirts for the event. Just in case.

Here is what we found:

8 P.M.: The party begins, and it looks as if it may be a success. The house is packed with men and women, all dancing furiously to a reggae band. The fraternity brothers are very excited. There is much howling, high-fiving, and head-butting. And, of course, a *lot* of heavy drinking.

8:20 P.M.: None of the fraternity brothers are talking to the women. "We get drunk first," they tell us. "It's easier that way."

8:35 P.M.: Somebody finally approaches a girl and attempts to seduce her by offering to show her the "secret handshake." She turns him down.

8:47 P.M.: The fraternity brothers decide that they will get drunk faster if they use a beer bong. A line forms and two kegs are finished off in less than ten minutes.

9:04 P.M.: The now very intoxicated fraternity brothers are shouting "Free Bird" at the reggae band. People are getting annoyed and leaving.

9:28 P.M.: The fraternity brothers take to the dance floor and start slam dancing with the women. More people leave.

9:55 P.M.: It is announced that the beer is gone. Everybody leaves.

9:59 P.M.: A few scared-looking pledges are sent out to get more beer. They are not allowed to wear pants. For whatever reason, the pledges agree.

10:11 P.M.: While waiting for the beer to arrive, the fraternity brothers are entertained by a guy named "Horse." He is a seven-foot, three-hundred-pound idiot who enjoys breaking bottles over his head. Everybody seems to be highly entertained by this. There is much head-butting and howling.

10:25 P.M.: The pledges have not yet returned with beer, so the house is searched for any traces of alcohol. A strange and foul-tasting concoction is created, consisting of vodka, prune juice, and Robitussin decongestant. The fraternity brothers drink it with enthusiasm.

10:32 P.M.:   The fraternity's president tells us that he hopes to change the negative image of frats. "This isn't just a place for sex and drinking," he says. "It's also a very supportive community that can teach guys how to work together as a team." He is wearing a "No Fat Chicks" t-shirt.

10:41 P.M.:   A guy who has passed out from too much alcohol is dragged onto the front porch, stripped naked, and urinated on. Everybody has a good laugh over this.

11:01 P.M.:   The pledges finally show up with the beer. There is much howling and high-fiving.

11:04 P.M.:   It is discovered that the pledges accidentally bought ginger beer. There is some discussion about going out for more beer, but this is quickly rejected because of lack of funds.

11:14 P.M.:   People are beginning to show up at the party again, and even, surprisingly, some women. Completely tanked at this point, the fraternity brothers make their moves. This consists mainly of pressing up against a woman and saying, "What's going on, baby?"

11:17 P.M.:   All of the women have left.

11:23 P.M.:   A clever fraternity brother spikes the ginger beer with bourbon, which causes most of the guests to get violently ill.

11:34 P.M.:   A half-naked fraternity brother enters from the upstairs dorm area and loudly announces that he got laid. There is much howling and high-fiving. When asked where the woman is, he insists that she left via the fire exit.

11:45 P.M.: The house pet, an ancient and tired-looking Doberman, has knocked over a table and is eating the chips and dip. The fraternity brothers cheer it on.

11:56 P.M.: A fraternity brother comes running in and says that two women are heading toward the house. There is much high-fiving and head-butting, until it's realized that it was just a false alarm.

12:09 A.M.: One of the fraternity brothers has gotten into a fistfight with the band. Although he eventually passes out, the band decides to leave.

12:12 A.M.: A small group of fraternity brothers are picked to go find some women.

12:14 A.M.: The remaining fraternity brothers drink what is left of the ginger beer and watch porn videos.

12:30 A.M.: An ambulance shows up. "Horse" has given himself a concussion after attempting to break a chair over his head.

12:38 A.M.: The search party returns with girls and a few bottles of generic rum.

12:42 A.M.: The president discovers that the girls are under-age and kicks them out. "We're not gonna go through *that* again," he says. "We've learned our lesson."

12:53 A.M.: Growing bored, the fraternity brothers decide to use the beer bong on the rum.

1:15 A.M.: The party is officially moved to the bathroom, as most of the fraternity brothers are now vomiting.

1:21 A.M.: A fraternity brother reveals a soiled pair of panties and everybody takes turns putting it on his head and going, "Whoa, baby!"

1:32 A.M.: The Doberman is drinking from one of the toilets. The fraternity brothers cheer it on.

1:40 A.M.: There is much howling, high-fiving, and head-butting, and then everybody passes out.

The Inevitable and Admittedly Tiresome Look at Safe Sex

Unfortunately, the casual sex of college is not all fun and unreturned phone calls. We are living in the nineties, an era where sexual diseases are more widespread than unsigned indie rock bands. You can't just go sticking your love-pump into any ol' hole without considering the consequences. Sex *is* dangerous these days, and if you insist on dancing the jig of promiscuity, you have to take the necessary steps to protect yourself.

And that means condoms.

Yeah, we know. You hate condoms. Well what of it? Who *doesn't* hate condoms? They're uncomfortable, they're awkward, they ruin the mood, and, more often than not, they give you about as much sensitivity as wrapping your penis in a Persian rug. But until a better solution comes along, you really don't have much choice.

If you're the stubborn type, you might argue that condoms aren't the best way of preventing sexual diseases. And you'd be right. According to the Centers for Disease Control and Prevention, the only way to completely protect yourself from STDs is by abstaining from sexual activity altogether. If you want to take that route, you're welcome to it. And while you're at it, why don't you try to stop breathing for a while too. It'd be just as easy.

The fine folks at the disease center also suggest engaging in sexual activities that don't involve vaginal, anal, or oral intercourse. And what exactly would *that* be? Dry-humping maybe? Hand-jobs? That might have worked for us in high school, but in the world of *adults,* we need something a little stronger to keep us happy.

Next to the idiotic suggestions of the CDC, condoms have been proven to provide the most sensible safe sex available. In a study done in Europe, the effectiveness of condoms was tested with a number of couples, some of whom had sexual diseases and some of whom did not. Among the couples who used condoms consistently, nobody became infected. But the couples who used condoms inconsistently became infected roughly 10 percent of the time. The lesson to be learned from these results is obvious. Namely, if you're going to participate in a study done in Europe, make sure that you're not just being suckered into getting an STD. We don't know what they pay the people who volunteer for those things, but it can't be worth getting a lot of running sores.

As simple as condoms are to use, most guys don't have a clue of what to do with them. We know that the rubber thingee goes on the penis, but that's about all we've been able to figure out. Condoms will only prevent STDs if you use them correctly, so it's important that you become more knowledgeable of how they work. Proper condom use should include the following steps:

- You should always use a latex condom. We don't know why exactly, but all the scientists say that latex is better. Don't use condoms that are made of sheepskin. Anybody who knows anything about safe sex says that sheepskin condoms don't provide any of the protection you need. But even if sheepskin condoms were effective, we probably wouldn't recommend them anyway. There's something about putting anything sheep-related next to your penis that has really creepy "farm-boy-looking-for-love" connotations.

• Put on the condom as soon as an erection occurs and before any sexual contact. In other words, if you put on a condom before you leave the apartment to pick up your date, you've used it *too soon.* But if you reach for a condom because it feels like you're ready to ejaculate, then you've used it *too late.*

• Use a new condom for each act of intercourse. To translate, this means that after you've used a condom once, you should *throw it away.* A lot of guys seem to think that condoms can be broken in like a piece of clothing. But unlike your favorite t-shirt, a condom does not get better or more comfy over time. Not only does repeated use make a condom useless, it's also really, really gross.

• Hold the tip of the condom and unroll it onto the erect penis, leaving some space at the tip. This extra space is for the sperm. You remember the sperm, don't you? That's the stuff you're trying to keep from going into your date. If sperm doesn't have anywhere to go, it'll panic and try to sneak down the side. Sperm, like any other living thing, has a healthy sense of self-preservation. The condom's purpose is to convince the sperm to stop its mad dash for the vagina. "What's your rush?" you're telling the sperm. "That egg isn't going anywhere. Why don't you chill out for a while and take a load off?" By the time the sperm realizes that it's been duped, the condom should be well out of harm's way.

• Withdraw from your partner immediately after ejaculation and remove the condom. Vaginas are like super-powered vacuum cleaners. If you give it half the chance, it will hang on to a condom for all its worth. Better men than you have played the condom tug-of-war with a vagina and lost, so don't think that you'll be any different. Get that condom out of there and at least thirty feet away from the vagina, and *then* you can snuggle with your honey.

Although condoms are a nuisance to use, they don't have to be boring. The trick to getting the most out of condoms is finding a style that's right for you. If you think that all condoms are pretty much the same, you're very mistaken. If you look a little farther than the corner drugstore, you'll discover that there are hundreds of different kinds of condoms out there, and they're all designed to make safe sex more interesting.

In the interest of keeping you, our delicate reader, as informed as possible, we have conducted intensive research of the vast variety of condoms available. Working day and night, we sampled every brand of condom we could find. Yes, this meant having a lot of sex. But in the interest of science and consumer awareness, we thought that it was worth it. And so, after exhaustive study and careful consideration, we give you this guide to the fascinating world of condoms.

Larger-sized: The biggest appeal of larger-sized condoms is that they're really fun to buy. "Excuse me," you say to the clerk. "Could I have a box of Magnums? Yes, that one there. The one marked 'Extra-Large.' " There is something undeniably gratifying about making a complete stranger think that you have an enormous penis. The problem is, not many guys have enough man meat to actually *fill* a Magnum. Although we'd all like to believe that we're hung like horses, there is nothing like a king-sized condom to bring your delusions of grandeur crashing down. The author who lost the coin toss and had to actually test the "Magnums" for this section is not what you'd call tiny in the groin department, but these condoms made him feel like a prepubescent boy. There was so much extra condom space left unused that his penis resembled a New Year's party favor. His girlfriend found this very amusing, and had a good laugh at his expense. He would recommend that unless you're absolutely certain that you need an extra-large condom, stay as far away from these things as possible.

Textured: In theory, textured condoms sound like a good idea. They come in a variety of styles—bumps, studs, or ribs—that are designed to give your partner plenty of satisfying friction. They're "For Her Pleasure," as the ads for Rough Rider condoms remind us. So we picked up a few boxes, feeling like the most generous boys in the world. If textured condoms were all it took to give a woman the Big O, we were more than eager to give it a shot. But when we put the condoms on, our enthusiasm quickly disappeared. There's something about seeing your penis covered in bumps that can be very unsettling. They're just too similar to some of those nasty STDs that we're trying to avoid by wearing condoms in the first place. Our partners were not any more impressed. "Your dick looks like a freakin' lizard," was one response. But despite the unsightly appearance of these condoms, we were confident that they would show their true colors when we put them to the test. Sure enough, they provided our lovely sex partners with lots of friction. But the friction did not result in the howls of ecstasy that we were hoping for. The sensation was described to us as not unlike rubbing sandpaper on the genitals. One of our girlfriends summed up her criticism best when she hollered, "For her pleasure *my ass!*" You get the idea. Unless you're in a spiteful mood, or your partner has sado-masochistic tendencies, you probably don't want to use these condoms with any regularity.

Sensitivity: These condoms are, without a doubt, our personal favorites. Sensitive condoms—otherwise known as Superthin, Ultrathin, or Very Thin—can make safe sex seem almost like *real* sex. They also have some of the best names. We picked up boxes of Excalibur, Kimono, Vis-À-Vis, Bareback, and Maxx just because we found their names so appealing. And when push comes to shove, these condoms will always deliver the goods. Some of them provide so much sensitivity that you'll keep pulling out to make sure that the damn things haven't fallen off. Although we tried almost every single brand on the market, our favorite was the more mainstream Lifestyles. We don't know what kind of secret formula Lifestyles uses, but we know that it works. Even our partners noticed a difference, and demanded that we use these condoms on a regular basis. So go buy lots of Lifestyles, and tell them that the authors of this book sent you. We know what you're thinking. No, Lifestyles did not pay us to say that. But if they decide to send us a lifetime supply of their brilliant condoms, well, let's just say that in the second printing of this book, the title will look a *lot* different.

Colored: Colored condoms allow you to paint your penis in shades of blue, orange, green, red, purple, yellow, or even black. We tried them all, and each was more disturbing than the next. Especially the black. Don't things on your body turn black if they've rotted and are about to fall off? You see what we're talking about? Guys have enough problems keeping an erection, we don't need the extra worry that our penises may, at any moment, crumble and disintegrate. The brighter colors may work for some guys, especially if they have some weird fantasy about being an alien stud. But personally, we were rather unnerved to see any color down there but our own natural skin tone.

Flavored or Scented: A few condom brands offer a wide array of flavors like strawberry and chocolate. But for the most part, you're going to have to be satisfied with mint. Why the majority of flavored condoms come only in mint is a mystery to us. Maybe it's because mint-flavoring creates the illusion that you're at the dentist. The whole point of flavored condoms is to make oral sex for women more pleasurable and safe. We can understand the safe part, but we have yet to meet a woman who is aroused by the taste of mint. Do we really think that we're fooling them? "Come on, honey. It'll freshen your breath *and* it helps fight cavities." We have a hard enough time getting our girlfriends to go down on us. Making our dicks taste like a Certs isn't going to convince any intelligent woman to change her mind. In fact, we don't know many women who will put their mouth around a condom anyway, even if it is minty-fresh. There's going to have to be a *lot* more people dropping dead from STDs before condoms and oral sex become congenial bedfellows.

Female Condoms: We were pretty excited to try these things. It was almost too good to be true. Finally, an annoying rubber thingie made just for *women*. As you might expect, female condoms aren't very popular among the fair sex. "Every other birth control device is made just for us," they say. "Why should we have to be responsible for wearing condoms as well?" We can understand their concern, but what they fail to realize is that no other birth control device is as irritating and uncomfortable as a condom.* If somebody came up with a pill that ensured safe sex, guys would be happy to take them. We're just not too keen on wrapping our dicks in surgical-strength Saran Wrap. It's about time that women should be forced to understand why guys hate condoms so much. Our girlfriends were pleasantly frustrated by the female condoms. "This sucks," one grumbled. "I can't feel a thing. I hate this. There's got to be a better way to practice safe sex than this." We could only smile. Sure, we weren't feeling much of anything either. But the thought that we were not alone made it more than worth it.

But even if you wear condoms regularly and use them correctly, this doesn't mean that you'll never get an STD. Condoms, sturdy little fuckers that they are, have been known to fail. There's always a chance that you're gonna end up with the Little Condom That Couldn't. Or maybe, just maybe, one day you'll forgo your sheath of love, and it'll turn out that it was the one time you needed a condom most. It happens. You can play by the rules most of the time, but all it takes is one screwup for you to qualify for the "Unluckiest Guy in the World" award. If only the lottery was this easy, huh?

Well, don't sweat it. Lots of people get STDs, and as most studies indicate, the vast ma-

---

* Except maybe the IUD, but nobody uses those anymore, do they?

jority of them are college students. The U.S. Department of Health and Human Services recently reported that as many as 12 million people in the United States alone get some kind of sexually transmitted infection each year. And roughly two thirds of those cases occur in people under twenty-five years of age while in college. With those kinds of odds, you should be surprised if you *don't* get an STD. It's almost like contracting an STD is a college rite of passage, like cramming for finals or changing your major at the last minute. It's just something that most college people do, and what the hell, you might as well join the fun.

Luckily, not many STDs are fatal. At most, they're terribly annoying and inconvenient. A quick needle in the ass can cure some of them, and the incurable ones can be managed, for the most part. But they still manage to make us feel depressed. There's nothing particularly glamorous or happy about them. When we think of STDs, we usually think of dirty old men in raincoats who hang around peep shows and relieve themselves in alleyways. Nobody wants to be known as "The Guy with the Clap." But considering how many of us get STDs, it would probably be in our collective best interests to take some of the stigma out of them and look on the bright side.

If you've discovered that you have an STD and it's left you feeling gloomy and despondent, take a moment and consider the good things about your sexual disease.

Making the Best of STDs

TYPE OF STD	LOOKING ON THE BRIGHT SIDE
Herpes	Those cute little blisters are sure to come back again and again, on a fairly regular basis. Think of it as your own built-in datebook. "Hey, look, I've got more sores. I guess rent's due."
Syphilis	A lot of really famous people have had it too, like Christopher Columbus, Oscar Wilde, Al Capone, Franz Schubert, and Meriwether Lewis. You're in good company.
Gonorrhea	It has been known to cause sterility, which kind of makes it a very inexpensive vasectomy. Congratulations, you managed to get for free what a lot of guys pay good money to get done professionally.
Trichomoniasis	Most infected men have no symptoms whatsoever, so it'll be years before you even remember that you have it.
Chlamydia	All that painful urination may help you finally overcome your drinking problem.
Hepatitis B	With symptoms like yellowish skin, foul breath, loss of appetite, and nausea, you could very well be mistaken for a stylish grunge-rock star.

Genital warts	Those cauliflower-like clusters may be painful and unsightly, but as far as sexual diseases go, this is pretty amateur stuff. Everybody knows that genital warts are nothing more than the "poor man's herpes."
Molluscum contagiosum	There's not much of a stigma attached to this disease, mostly because nobody seems to know what the hell it is.

✳ Abortion Etiquette ✳

As we've clearly established by now, birth control is everyone's responsibility. No excuses, no I-was-drunks, no guilty-foot-shufflings and hangdog looks; there is positively no excuse for not using the best protection money can buy for your little soldier.

The problem with this familiar refrain is that it fails to take into account what lazy, thoughtless slugs most of us are. If you disagree, and think this is an overpessimistic view of human beings, apply the iron-clad rhetoric of safer sex to communal living: Take the *a priori* truth, "Condom use is everyone's responsibility," and contrast it with the immortal words, "The dishes are everyone's responsibility." This is another big truth. A sink full of moldering crockery is a *bad thing,* and it shouldn't happen. You absolutely have to wash up after every meal from now on. No excuses, no exceptions. And yet, and yet . . . somehow the kitchen turns into a full-blown biohazard, and nobody knows how it happened. Accusations are made, fingers are pointed, and the whole thing ends in tears and moldy plates.

In fact, your authors have come to the conclusion that any time someone uses the phrase "everyone's responsibility," they're dooming us all, as well as whatever it was we were supposed to be responsible about: The bathroom is everyone's responsibility; the kitty litter is everyone's responsibility; the poor are everyone's responsibility; and elected officials are, God help us, everyone's responsibility.

So, given the abysmal record we have with huge, important things that we really ought to be paying attention to—no excuses, no exceptions, no evasions!—it's very possible you and your partner will experience an unplanned pregnancy.

Sends a bolt of ice down your spine just thinking about this, doesn't it? Makes you want to curl up and make the world go away. If you're ever confronted with that terrible, defining moment, you'll probably wish there really were adults who would clean up after your mess. Unfortunately, as of that exact moment, *you* are the adult, no matter how much you don't want to be.

As soon as your partner is sure she's with child, you're faced with very few choices. (Actually, to be precise, *she's* faced with the choices, and your only legal role is to go along for the ride.) Due to the pathetic, primitive state of late-twentieth-century medicine, your only options are to abort the pregnancy or have the child. Although neither one may be terribly appealing, that's it, that's the whole enchilada. Someday, when medicine has been dragged kicking and screaming out of the Victorian age, you'll have more choices, but for now that's it.

If your partner chooses the abortion route, the only gentlemanly thing to do is support the decision, and help her in any way you can. However, you'll be plunging into some murky ethical waters. Abortion is a fraught issue in America, with a lot of truly loud people lining up on both sides of the divide. Since your authors have zero wisdom to offer on the subject, we thought we'd at least present a quick summary of the standard arguments used by pro-choice and pro-life groups, to help you decide where you stand on the subject:

> *Standard pro-life argument:* Abortion is murder, no matter what phase the pregnancy is in, since even a tiny group of dividing cells has the potential of life.
>
> *Problem:* If potential is the measure of what's alive and what isn't, then each sperm cell is capable of becoming a human being, and we murder millions of children-to-be when we jerk off. If we accept the "potential" argument, masturbation is genocide, and oral sex often ends in mass cannibalism.

> *Standard pro-choice argument:* A fetus is not a fully-fledged human being until birth, and therefore is not "killed" when its life is ended.
>
> *Problem:* To award humanity at birth seems much too generous. Most people we know weren't really human beings until they suffered at least one major career failure and three broken hearts. Even then, some of them weren't very good at it. If we wait around for people to become human beings, abortion will be legal until the twentieth birthday, if not later.

Ultimately, of course, it doesn't matter what you think. Until that hazy day in the future when you'll be able to avail yourself of convenient, 100 percent effective birth control, or offer to carry the child yourself, you have no real say in the matter. You can express your feelings to your partner, of course, and this will have roughly the same weight and power as the average United Nations resolution—which is to say, zilch, *nada,* nothing. If she wants to carry the pregnancy to term, she will. If she decides to abort, she will. You had your vote when you poked your prick in the nearest inviting orifice without a condom, or when the condom broke, or when you fell for the one about a safe time of the month, or when her birth control pills conked out, or whatever.

And on that fateful day when you're agonizing over what's going to happen to you and your lady love, remember we told you—and we said it very sternly, mind you, shaking our finger, frowning, and getting on our highest horse—that birth control is everyone's responsibility.

Just like keeping the bathroom clean, yard work, and world hunger.

Homo You Don't (Valuable Pointers on Uncertain, Ambiguous, and Flip-Flopping Sexuality)

Now that we've got heavy, serious topics such as STDs out of the way, we can move on to the other pressing issue that will confront you in college. At some point or another, you're going to be at a happenin', phat house party, and you'll be shaking your booty with a woman who seems interested in you, of all people. And even as you go for refills from the keg back in the kitchen, surrounded by thick-necked frat boys who haven't budged from the source of beer since the party started, you're going to confront yourself with that most terrifying and soul-searching question: *If I'm not gay, why am I such a good dancer?*

And even if you go home with that lusty lady, and even if you prove your heterosexuality to yourself four times in rapid succession, you're still going to be left staring up at the ceiling of her dorm room, thinking about that 10 percent number. If it's true that one tenth of the population is light in the loafers, shouldn't you at least consider color-coordinating and reading *Details* with an eye for the

 not-very-subtle "alternative lifestyle" references?

First thing, don't get all worked up about it. If you should discover that you are gay, you can look forward to greater earning potential, finer clothing, higher intellectual regard, and a slew of porn films featuring perfectly built boy toys who will have you running to the nearest Nautilus machine out of sheer physical self-hatred. It's not such a bad life, all told.

But second, don't forget that you're in college, and sexual experimentation is the name of the game. You didn't get wigged out the first time you tried doggie-style, now did you? And what about the sorority sister who wanted to play with hot fudge and whipped cream? Meaning to say, even if you indulge in some naughtiness, it doesn't mean that you're planning on making hot fudge sundaes for the rest of your active sexual life.

But for those of you who have to bite your nails and wonder whether or not you're driving on the left-hand side of the road, here are a few signposts that will tell you where you are on the gender-bending superhighway:

THE TOP 10 REASONS YOU MAY SUSPECT YOU'RE GAY

Dressing better than the other men you know	This doesn't say much, since men pay all-too-little attention to their clothing in the first place. The only time to worry is when you go to a happenin' dance club and notice that you're dressed better than the fashion hounds, or if you start planning themes in your wardrobe. The day you decide to dress as your favorite character from *The Great Gatsby,* you have crossed an important line.
Affinity for show tunes and "original cast recordings"	Several of our gay friends have objected to this category as "too clichéd." However, when pressed, they admitted freely that enough gay men enjoy show tunes to rule out chance. So if you find yourself humming themes from *Carousel* and *Showboat* on a frequent basis, then yes, it's time to question your sexuality.
Affinity for Judy Garland, Bette Midler, or Barbra Streisand	There are at least a hundred different theories as to why some gay men bond to images of powerful female entertainers. We don't have any new ones, but maybe you do. Hmmmm?
A lot of women tell you that you're their "best friend"	This is a deadly situation that is not, we repeat, *not* limited to budding homosexuals. The "best friend" syndrome also happens to geeks, mama's boys, wimps, and girlie-men. If you aren't gay, the rest of your options are downhill.

Dorm room/student apartment is not a dump	Having a neat living space in college can mean only one of three things: You're a young Republican, an ROTC cadet, or a gay man. "All of the above" is an acceptable, if confusing, answer.
Becoming muscular and/or "fit"	Simple test: If, under any circumstance, you have a "washboard" stomach, prepare for major life changes.
Quality hair care	If you use three conditioners, hair gel, a good dye job twice a month, and you're on a first-name basis with a hairdresser, odds are that you are just a vain son of a bitch. If, on the other hand, you attend your coif with marginally more care than your average Joe, queerness is a possibility.
You came from a small town to a big city	No one can explain this one to our satisfaction. Is there something innately homoerotic about small towns? If so, why haven't Norman Rockwell paintings become fetish items? Why isn't *The Andy Griffith Show* a staple of the bar scene? Mysteries abound.
Hanging around or enrolling in the theater department	There's nothing inherently queer about being interested in theater. If, however, you are any good at all, your odds of gayness increase exponentially.
Dancing too damn well	You're on dangerous ground. If you're attached to heterosexuality, it's time to volunteer for the Religious Right group of your choice, and read one year's worth of back issues of *Guns and Ammo*.

None of these items, by themselves, should be enough to tell you that you're gay. However, if you find yourself tallying up seven or more of the above points, and saying, *Hmm, that seems to apply,* then you've got a whole lot of issues to confront. Very *serious* issues, mind you, such as how to come out to your friends, how and when to tell your parents,

how to meet like-minded people, and where you fit into the gay community, if you fit in at all. These are tough questions that are really hard to make funny, and since we're under contract to write a funny book, we're going to skip them. Besides, if you're dating men, then the rest of us can only envy you; men are a lot simpler than women.

We aren't sure why there are so many books about dating written for women in the first place. In three sentences we can say everything you'll ever need to know about dating a man. In order, they are:

- Men like sex a lot.
- They are suckers for flattery, no matter how outrageous.
- They lie.

There, wasn't that painless? So if you should come to realize that you're gay, you've got it easy. Men are no problem. Flatter 'em, fuck 'em, and don't believe a word they say. You'll get along great.

Lesbian Chic

Trust us, you're going to run into the sapphic scene while on campus. Maybe it will be a woman you know who decides to only date women for her sophomore year. Or perhaps it will be in the form of a girlfriend who speaks at great length about her fantasies of other women. Or maybe you'll get involved in a sexual situation that involves two girls who are more interested in each other than you, as happened to one of the authors, except the whole thing was kind of embarrassing and humiliating, since the two-girl thing had been a standard fantasy since adolescence, and he'd wanted it to go better, and he felt terribly disillusioned, I mean, come on, how can you have two girls in bed and not really enjoy it, so on top of everything he felt like a capital "L" loser, so he'd rather not say which one he is *if you don't mind all that terribly.*

As we were saying, the odds are quite good that while you're spending all of that money to learn how to go to college, you'll encounter lesbianism, or one of her close relatives. While boys stand around the pool of sexual experimentation, dipping our toes in the water, shivering, and wondering if maybe we should just go in up to our waist, college women have been diving in with gusto. A truly disconcerting number of women consider the girl-girl experience a rite of passage reserved for the university. "My one regret," a Smith College graduate told us, "is that I never slept with a woman. If you're going to, that's the time to do it."

We're not sure what true-blue lesbians think of all this experimentation, although Lisa Cox, promoter for Girls in the Night, summed it up nicely when she said, "We're like bell-bottoms. We're a novelty and everybody wants us. When we stop being so chic, you're going to see a lot of lesbians going on 'Oprah' talking about how some straight woman used them." Which would make total sense, except that so many women play around in college that we're forced to wonder how many real lesbians are getting "used," or whether instead it's mostly dabblers playing with dilettantes.

But therein lies the secret appeal of part-time lesbianism. It's more fun than calculus, and less inconvenient than attending a rally or march. And while students can support ethnic minorities, the poor, and the disenfranchised, it's impossible to become one of them for the weekend. The campus lesbian craze has a sort of user-friendly, no-strings convenience that makes everything okay, and darn middle-class.

And for whatever reason, this form of sexuality is less stigmatized in our society than boy-boy love. It's as if the whole nation sided with Sean Connery, who said, "The idea of two men kissing I find shocking in a sexual way. But the idea of two women embracing, it looks somehow all right." And the lesbian thing is so convenient and inclusive, you can even join in by changing your alias at the campus computer center to a more feminine nom de e-mail. Once you've changed JBowen@ucmas.edu to the more provocative Fire-Vixen@ucmas.edu, you're free to pursue your very own lesbian love online. Of course, the majority of Internet users are male, which means that the hundreds of people who crowd America Online's Lesbian Biker Chat Forum are also probably male, which means that you've got a lot of men loving men . . . as women. Which leads us right back to the fact that lesbianism makes everything more acceptable. Even—*ahem*—the most manly forms of one-handed typing. As Howard Stern so rightly put it, "You cannot go wrong with lesbians."

If deciding whether or not you're a male homosexual is a soul-searching question that requires months of introspection and repeated listening to Morrisey CDs, the lesbianism thing is a no-brainer. When it comes to dykes, the entire body politic woke up one morning and said, "Me, too." If a woman who piques your interest announces she's a lesbian, it's not unfair for you to ask for an estimate of how long.

Of course, if she's really made a lifestyle switch, you're out of luck, and it's best to move your affections elsewhere. Or she may be moving toward that tricky beast known as bisexuality.

Anything That Moves

We can't help but question the motives of someone who makes a commitment to bisexuality. And we aren't talking about the folks who spend some time wavering before settling on their life course—it's an established fact that most gay men have experimented with women at some time or another, which seems only natural. And we're told that a lot of straight men did some playing-doctor with other boys during adolescence, only to lie about it later. We wouldn't know anything about that. Nope. Couldn't tell you the first thing. We're not saying we disapprove, mind you, we're just saying it wasn't us. Must have been somebody else. Maybe somebody who *looked* like one of us.

Anyway, as we were saying, there's something strange about people who make a long-term choice to fuck anything that moves. For one thing, they're doubling the number of people who get to reject them, which is very odd. Being brushed off by one gender is bad enough for most folks.

And then there are the bisexuals we've known personally.

We might as well admit that both of us worked in the theater for years.* Spitznagel is a wise man, and has dropped it entirely, but Brendan still goes back from time to time, for reasons he can explain to no one. But one cannot survive in the theater without making gay friends. A lot of gay friends. And the funny thing is, they're remarkably similar to straight friends; some are loyal, wonderful people, while others are pathetic excuses for human beings, consuming valuable oxygen and food. The ratio of good to evil seems on a par with anywhere else.

But the bisexuals we've known are on a different wavelength. Some have been so horny that *everything* gets them going, while others have been terminally unable to make up their minds.

A few have been both.

And that's about it.

We know, we know, this is very unfair. We're speaking from personal experience, not a big demographic survey.† But while some gay men and lesbians have been loyal, trustworthy friends, there's just something unsettled about bisexuals. Although they have nice rhetoric about "loving people instead of gender," it doesn't quite add up. Unconditional love sounds great on paper, but in real life it always ends up meaning Collectivist Socialism or Ecstasy.

Men and women have specific bits of plumbing. You can fetishize the penis, or you can fixate on the vagina. (It goes without saying that everybody loves a good butt and a pretty face.) But the bisexuality thing seems to be about nonspecific erotic feelings, a

---

* Yes, this means we're probably gay.

† For the record, Brendan has been on semifriendly terms with five male and eight female bisexuals. Spitznagel has crossed paths with a grand total of one and a half (the half being an undecided bisexual). So we're not claiming to be the Census Bureau, okay?

sort of haziness of the libido. It's as though you were playing Monopoly and someone insisted on being both the Top Hat *and* the Sports Car.

Bisexuals have talked about this a lot, and they seem to have a legitimate gripe. They complain that neither the straight nor the gay community really accepts them, and they're right, we don't.

And if our goal is to be as inclusive and broad-minded as possible, we shouldn't go telling people to pick a preference. *Hey,* we should say, *take your time. Shop around. Try before you buy. Don't worry, we'll wait for you by the checkout counter.* But your authors really aren't all that broad-minded. In fact, we have narrow, stunted minds, and there seems a world of difference between someone who knows what he or she likes, and dabbles on the side, and a person committed to not committing.

But we could be way off-base on this one. The lesbian chic thing is already past its peak, and bisexuality may be all the rage before you can say "sexual preference as fashion accessory." Everybody on campus will "love people as people," and grumpy contrarians like us will be consigned to the reduced-price clothing depot of history. Everybody will hug everybody a whole lot, and love will reign supreme. Nobody will be gay or straight unless they're really pushy about it, and the Book of Love will be rewritten along gender-neutral editorial guidelines.

Nah. It'll never work. Odds are that full-time bisexuals will more or less always be a hard-to-get-along-with subminority. If the rules get loosened to the point where every woman feels safe sleeping with another woman from time to time, and straight boys have no problem with the occasional friendly bout of knob-polishing, the vast majority of people are still going to know what they like.

In other words, people will feel free to play the Top Hat when the spirit moves them, but at the end of the day they'll go back to the little pewter Schnauzer.

Where All da Women At?

(Meeting and Greeting)

After college, dating becomes a much more complex and frustrating endeavor. For one thing, it isn't nearly as easy to find women. As freaky as most college women are, they aren't too difficult to track down. All you have to do is go to class or hang out at the local bar and you're bound to bump into one of them. And unlike the real world, you're guaranteed to have something in common with them. You're both going to college, the *same* college, so you already have something to talk about. Even guys with a limited imagination can ask "What's your major?" and probably do all right. It's a win-win situation that, sadly, does not exist outside the comfy confines of higher learning.

The problem with finding women in the outside world is that there are a lot more of them and they're spread out all over the place. It can seem like an impossible task, but rest assured, the woman of your dreams is out there somewhere. If you're willing to do a little legwork and explore all the options, you may be able to track her down. The best thing you can do is visit the locales where single women are most likely to congregate. There are many possibilities, and not all of them will be as lucrative as you may think. But lucky for you, we've already done your research. We've investigated some of the most popular places and events used to pick up women, in an attempt to discover which offered the highest rate of successful matchups. Here's what we found:

Bars

ADVANTAGES: Low lights and beer goggles make her un-likely to react to your appearance, and these atmospheric conditions will also make her more attractive to you. For the introduction-impaired, buying a drink provides an easy—if clichéd—mode of entry. If you're both stupid, you can always commune by the jukebox, and bond over statements such as, "Wow, you love No Doubt? *I* love No Doubt!"

DISADVANTAGES: Most women travel to bars as herd ani-mals, and you can expect the packs' defenses to be up. If they begin growling, *do not* raise your hackles, display your claws, fan your tail plumage, or puff your neck sac. They're already wise to those tricks. Frankly, when in a bar, they're wise to *every* trick. A bar is to meeting women what "knock-knock" is to joke telling, so any attempt to talk will be construed as a hack-neyed pickup. No matter how subtle and charming you think you're being, it's coming off with the elegance of an epileptic giraffe on ice skates.

CONCLUSION: A man on the make in a bar makes women feel that same sense of warmth and security they get when be-ing followed out of a car park at 2 A.M.

Your local tavern is for drinking, playing pool, and grunting at the moon. As for everything else, a great big Go Easy to ya.

Clubs

ADVANTAGES: They're big, they're loud, they're hip, and they're chock full of beautiful bulimics. The music is so loud that you don't have to worry about conversational skills, or niggling details like her name. Park yourself at a table and try to look cool, or get out on the floor and try to look cool, or stand in line for the bathroom and try to look cool. It doesn't matter who you are, what you do, or whether you speak the Queen's English, so long as you reek of all things cool. If you have friends with eight-syllable last names and monthly arrangements with the local police, you can also get a VIP pass, which cements your coolness, you super-cool dude, you.

DISADVANTAGES: Who really wants to date an eating-disordered model wanna-be? Odds are she actually works in retail, and that she has more relationship "issues" than you can shake a stick at. And while we're at it, don't go shaking sticks, since God alone knows what repressed memory that will dredge up. It comes down to a basic issue: Do you really want to pursue the short-lived, fragile beast known as "cool"? Clubs turn into a big game of pecking order, and if you're very unlucky you'll be at the top one day. And as you're being ushered into the throbbing ex-warehouse, with a bevy of speed-freak, jail-bait cuties hanging on every twitch of your Marlboro, you're going to wonder why you didn't get a life instead.

CONCLUSION: Clubs will do the trick if your standards are low. But why not save the money you're blowing on the Armani Exchange and crystal meth, and spend it on more creative habits like auto theft or narcolepsy?

Work

ADVANTAGES: Try before you buy. You get to know her, she gets to know you, and you both have a frame of reference that doesn't include beer breath. Although she may still suspect that you are a woman-hating serial killer, the fact that you behave normally at work may allay her fears for a while. And to top it off, according to a study conducted at Arizona State University by psychologist Sanford Braver, the more handsome you are, the less likely you are to ever be accused of misconduct. The beautiful, it would seem, can do no wrong.

DISADVANTAGES: The study also discovered that if the man was unattractive, he couldn't say "Hello" too often without it being construed as sexual harassment. The moral of this story is clear: Life ain't fair, especially when you're ugly. Another problem is breaking up, since you're still going to be seeing her around the office. Unless you enjoy strained smiles and cold stares, think twice before shopping in the company store.

CONCLUSION: Obviously, if you aren't as good-looking as you think you are, it's firing and fining time for your sorry ass, no matter how subtle your moves. Sure, there's been a backlash against sexual harassment suits in the last couple of years, but who's to say there won't be a backlash against the backlash? And then a backlash against all of the previous backlashes? With sexual politics moving so quickly, by the time we've noticed the trend, added it to a new version of this book, waited while our publisher consults the bones of his ancestors, and gotten the thing into bookstores, it'll already be one backlash too late. For now, we'll just say that the workplace is a decent place to meet women, sort of, depending on the time of year and what kind of hair day you're having. We'd say more, but we feel a backlash coming.

Parties

Parties can be the best of times and the worst of times. Since there are so many different sorts, we're going to break them down into subsections, so you might more easily decide which ones work for you:

TYPE	ADVANTAGES	DISADVANTAGES	CONCLUSION
Small parties	Everyone knows everybody else, and the atmosphere is relaxed and mellow.	You already know everybody there. *Yawn.*	Good for seducing someone you already know, bad for meeting new people.
Big parties	Lots of mixing and music. Also, the free-flowing alcohol lubricates social intercourse.	If you're shy, or worse, boring, you're gonna get lost in the mix. And with so many interesting people around, don't expect her to give you a second chance.	Be interesting or die.

Small parties that turn into big parties	The press of too many people in a small place makes for lots of up-close intimacy.	The hooch may run out, as may your date.	These offer the perfect chance to look deeply into her eyes and suggest you leave for someplace less crowded . . . like maybe her place.
Big parties that turn out to be small parties	Fewer people to horn in on the person you're talking to.	Everyone is kind of depressed and quiet, since nobody showed up.	It's a good time to suggest that you go someplace more happening . . . like maybe her place.
Work parties	Lots of people you know, as well as their friends and mates. Good mix of the familiar and the new.	Everyone's either someone you work with or dating someone you work with. Life sucks.	See previous listing ("WORK").
Public parties	Tons of new people, all out for a good time.	Who wants to pay for a party with strangers? Unless it's a well-organized event, you're going to feel like a big ol' loser	Marginally better than a bar, but still not a very good place to meet women.

Clique parties	Similar advantages to those of a small party, only with subdivisions.	Since the guests are all huddled in their little social groups, nobody gets to meet anybody new. Also, there's the nagging feeling that your clique isn't as hip as that one over there.	It's a good time to suggest that you go someplace less snotty and segregated . . . like maybe her place.

Weddings

ADVANTAGES: People are relaxed. Romance is in the air. The champagne is flowing. She's dressed up. You're dressed up. Everybody's feeling good. Odds are one of you has a hotel room. By the time of the reception, everyone's gotten past the jitters of watching a friend get hitched, and is feeling mellow and good about relationships. Oodles of excuses to introduce yourself without seeming like a freak or a pervert. The labyrinthine defenses of the average woman are at an all-time low. And like we said, one or both of you has a hotel room, right nearby, and let's go on up, just, you know, to talk and stuff, and what room number are you again?

DISADVANTAGES: Somebody's uncle will drink too much and vomit on a table. Trust us on this one, and try not to be there when it happens—

the splatter radius is larger than you think. You should also try to be across the room when somebody's father vomits on a table. But it's okay to sit at the table where somebody's aunt has passed out face-down in a slowly spreading stain of red wine. If you pat her on the back occasionally and say, "There, there, it'll be okay," you can even score points by seeming compassionate.

CONCLUSION: Hands-down the best place to meet women, assuming it's a friend of yours getting married. However, if it's some sort of family obligation event, be prepared to vomit on a table or pass out. If you really want to drink without getting sick, try limiting yourself to simple mixed drinks such as vodka gimlets or rum and Coke, as it is an established fact that all catering companies get their wine from ex-Soviet satellite states. Two glasses of the stuff and you'll swear you can see the music.

Cyberspace

ADVANTAGES: You get to zoom around the information superhighway, and you can't help but feel hip doing anything with the prefix "cyber-" attached. Lots of people online seem to be friendly, and an awful lot of them are named LuvBeast@penetration.com. How can a boy resist? Should you hit it off with someone, you get all of the advantages of those old Victorian romance-by-letter stories. There's something sweet about sending note after note to a lover you've never met in the flesh. Some even claim that e-mail romance is purer than everything else we've listed in this section, since you're more mind-to-mind when you write.

DISADVANTAGES: If you can't type quickly, you're screwed. And forget about your corporeal charm, since none of it is captured in ASCII.* If you've got a voice like Barry White and a body like a gymnast, it doesn't matter; she can't hear or see you. Also, you should stop and consider how many of those women you meet online are really men. It's disconcerting how many of us, when offered the chance, will digitally cross-dress. We know a guy who conducted a steamy lesbian love affair online, only to discover that his paramour was also male. This makes for beautiful poetic justice, but not very good dating. There is a reason that net-savvy people ask if you've made an "eye-D" of your online lover. And even if she isn't male, she may be—how shall we say it nicely?—not your *physical* type. The unluckier of your authors (as per usual, he'd rather not identify himself due to raw embarrassment), after several months of romantic correspondence with a lady in another city, discovered that the object of his desire was rather plain-looking. Despite his intellectual conviction that appearances shouldn't matter, he found that they do. More than he'd care to admit.

CONCLUSION: Although the number of female users is growing, the Internet continues to be something of a boy's club. This means that a woman who goes fishing on the net can be choosy, while you join a cast of thousands. We, your humble authors, don't like those odds. For all that we hear the stories about people meeting and falling in love on the net, we suspect that the majority of digital romance consists of men masturbating to the speed-typing of *other* men in America Online's BiFem4Fem chat room. Do not trust *Wired,* Nicholas Negroponte, the E.F.F., or

---

* "ASCII" is the itty-bitty letter set that you're allowed to transmit over the Internet proper. It doesn't allow for accents, curly quotes, long dashes, umlauts, or anything beyond the most basic alphabet and the occasional piece of child pornography. This is why you are unlikely to meet any typography babes while cruising the net.

any of those shameless, self-promoting, futurist hucksters on this one. When it comes to finding your true love, old ways are the best ways.

Conversing and Impressing

So now you know where to find them, the next step is to convince them to talk to you. The first impression is very important, but not impossible to master. A lot of it is just common sense, which admittedly most guys don't possess. But just follow these five simple rules and you should be able to conduct a successful dialogue with a woman without fear of instant rejection.

1. Get a life. Have something to talk about. Whether it be your job or your friends or even something you saw on TV last night, have at your disposal some nugget of information that you think is interesting and that you would like to share with her. Sure, it's nice if you listen to her, but there are only so many times that you can ask "What do *you* think?" before you will be expected to say something on your own.

2. Make eye contact. Trust us, it's more difficult than it sounds. Don't look at her breasts, or her legs, or her hair, or the woman seated at the other end of the bar, or the guy who just walked out of the bathroom who you think might be a friend from college. Look at her eyes. Eye contact is the best way to say, "I am listening to you." Coincidentally, it is also the best way to say, "I challenge your standing as leader of the herd," but that's another issue altogether.

3. Keep away from controversial subject matter. Your first conversation with a woman is not the best time to debate political beliefs. Stay on subjects that you can both agree on, like your favorite colors and what shapes clouds make. A harmless comment like "I hate sitting next to a crying baby on a plane" can evolve into a heated discussion of child care reform and abortion rights. Next thing you know, you've got a ranting demagogue on your hands, demanding to know whether you support a woman's right to choose.

4. Bring your paperwork. Unless you can prove, with proper documentation, that you are disease-free, over twenty-one, have a job, and have never been convicted of a felony, most women will not even give you the time of day. Carry the required paperwork with you at all times, as well as a picture ID for further verification.

5. Do not have a mustache. Enough said on that subject.

Fuck You
. . . I Want a Hug

Showing Her Your Tough Side *and* Your Sensitive Side

Just as us guys are attracted to the madonna/whore complex, women want a man who combines the best of both worlds. They want us to be tough yet sensitive, aggressive yet gentle. They want a beau who can cry on cue but isn't averse to mopping the floor with some guy's face, if necessary. But if you're going to convince her that you have a good *and* bad side, you need to be on your toes. Here are a few examples that will help you get started:

SOCIAL SCENARIO	YOUR SENSITIVE SIDE	YOUR TOUGH SIDE
Dinner at an expensive restaurant	Order wine and propose a toast "to us."	Order a steak, make it raw, and ask if you can kill the bull with your bare hands.
Meeting her parents	Compliment her mother on her good looks and thank them both for raising such a wonderful daughter.	Wrestle her father to the floor, break one of his fingers, and then loudly denounce his masculinity.
A night at the opera	Cry during the sad scenes, nod thoughtfully during the rest.	During the final number, organize a mosh pit. Then rush the stage and head-butt the lead soprano.
Hanging with her friends	Appear delighted to meet them, ask about their careers, and seem genuinely interested in what they have to say.	Smash a bottle over a table and threaten to cut any of her guy friends if they give you any guff.
First sexual encounter	Play soft, romantic music, slowly undress her, and whisper sweet nothings into her ear.	When you reach orgasm, shout "That's one for the Gipper!" Then drop to the floor and bench-press her stereo.

But Is She Right For You?

At first she may seem perfect. She's pretty, she's smart, and she likes you. And that's fine, if all you're looking for is a little pleasant dinner conversation. But is she someone you could spend some serious time with, and maybe even commit to a long-term relationship? Too many men forget that they are not the only ones required to audition for love. Sure, you must learn to accept *Melrose Place,* chick flicks, and putting down the toilet seat. But does she share *your* interests as well? To find out if she has what it takes to keep your attention for the long haul, ask her to take this short and simple quiz. If she answers "yes" to any or all of these questions, you may very well have found a soul mate.

1. Have you seen the original Star Wars *trilogy?*

2. Do you know which of the Three Stooges coined the phrase "woo-woo-woo"?

3. Can you hold your whiskey, or at least respect a man who can?

4. Do you know the difference between a layup and a foul shot?

5. Can you hum a few bars from any song recorded by Kiss? ("Beth" does not count.)

6. Can you discuss, without mockery, the career of David Hasselhoff?

7. Do you possess the knowledge necessary to check the oil in a car?

8. *Have you ever sat through an entire screening of* Scarface? *If not, would you be willing to do so if necessary?*

9. *Can you identify the difference between a* G.I. *Joe action figure and a* G.I. *Joe doll with kung-fu grip?*

10. *Do you appreciate the subtle charms of a concealed handgun?*

11. *Does the name "Seka" mean anything to you?*

Everything I Ever Really
Needed to Know About
Seduction I Learned from
Submarine Warfare

So you've met her, and much to your surprise, she's still talking and/or e-mailing you.
Where do you go from here? How do you
move from "Hello" to "Don't stop, baby,
keep going, do it to me, yeah, you know
how I like it"?

It's hard to say, and harder still to
codify. One woman's Casanova is another's Quasimodo. But whatever you do, don't think you need to have it all. Sure, it would be
nice to wake up one day and be rich, handsome, funny, self-depre-
cating, talented, and hung like a grizzly, but it's also unnecessary. A
few shortcomings never stopped a determined rascal. Take, for example, a few of the standardized hunks of the late twentieth century:

HUNK	OBVIOUS PROBLEM(S)	COMPENSATES BY . . .
Sean Connery	old, fat, beats wives	being a movie star
Fabio	vapid	causing breast envy
Bill Gates	dweeby, freakish	taking over the world
Patrick Stewart	old and bald	owning a starship
Keanu Reeves	vapid	causing cheekbone envy
Henry Kissinger	old and ugly	*almost* taking over the world
JFK Jr.	insipid	being a Kennedy

What these men are doing right is working within their limitations. Let this be your inspiration, your guide, your mantra. If you've got a beer gut, work your smarts. If you haven't got smarts, play off your wealth. If you haven't got money, use your humor. It's rule number one of seduction:

1. Work with what you've got. In other words, forget your shortcomings and play off the good stuff.

2. Make your filthy intentions clear. After all, you don't want to hear the dreaded words: "You're my best friend in the whole world." If she ever starts talking about you as a "friend" to your face, you're dead meat. Don't let this happen to you. Exude danger and excitement, dress better, talk constantly about sex, do whatever it takes, but don't let her think you just want to be her bud. (An im-

portant exception to this rule is the group of
men who use friendship as their main seduction technique. You know the type:
They have a harem of female companions
who need either Daddy or Brother. They
wait until one of the women is having a cri-
sis before closing for the kill. Unfortunately, this seems to backfire as often as it
works, since the kind of woman who's

looking for a father-figure has her own set of problems and pecu-
liarities. Six out of ten dating experts say: *Don't play Daddy unless
you're ready to give a good spanking.)*

3. Be a nuclear submarine. Since they lack windows, subs use
two forms of sound to gather information about their surroundings:
Passive sonar is where they listen to ambient noise, and try to guess
what it all means; active sonar is when they go *ping!* and use the
sound's reflection to map the terrain. The latter is risky, since it reveals the sub's position, but it yields better information. When you
shut up and listen to a woman, you're being a quiet sub. You're ac-
cepting her perspective, letting her guide the conversation, and not
putting your crew at risk. This works if she's as forceful as a tsunami,
and making her intentions very clear. But since honest lust is much
more rare than the dance of deception, we recommend using *active*
sonar. Send out little pings in the form of flirtatious statements and
good eye contact. The echo will tell you everything you need to
know. Is she smiling and biting her lip when you hold her gaze? If
so, send out another ping. Remember, positioning is everything in
undersea warfare. Is she facing you and directing the conversation
your way? Ping at will, laddie—she's a friendly ship! Or is she turning away, even slightly, and trying to talk to someone else? If so,
dive, dammit, *dive!* Run silent, run deep! Don't send out any more
signals; it'll just reveal your location, and she's a bogey. That captain
is not going down on your ship.

4. Run away! If she's giving you the heave-ho, don't fight, go. The only place where chasing a reluctant damsel works is in romance novels, which is part of the reason those things aren't sold to men. It should also be noted that if she's sending you mixed signals, you should walk away. Sure, you might be able to bed her, but do you really want to? A woman who's mixed up about flirting is usually confused about a lot of other things too, and that kind of grief you don't need. Come morning, you'll be oh-so-glad you didn't.

5. Or make your move. If, on the other hand, you're getting a lot of clear, warm responses, it's time to be decisive. Oh sure, it's scary. And nobody wants to look like a fool. But someone's going to have to tip the conversation from almost to definitely, and it's probably going to be you, current sexual politics notwithstanding. Whether it's your seventh date or your first encounter, there will come a moment when things are teetering on the brink, and all that's required is a gentle push. There's no need to get frisky with your hands or tongue, but make a gesture that is definitely, unmistakably sexual. Do it slowly, giving her plenty of time to back off—if you go for a kiss, don't jam your face into hers as though you were going for a head-butt. Remember, you're a submarine, a very stealthy creature, and this is the Big Ping. Your sonar operator should be on red alert.

6. Never stop listening. Oh-ho, so you've kissed? And it went well? Good, wonderful, fabulous, but don't go thinking you're out of danger. Smooching only establishes interest. There are going to be a lot of crucial moments after that first one, and after every ping you'd better be listening as though your life depended on it. How does she react to a light touch on the neck? On the shoulder? On the thigh? Sure, she may make it easy for you, and say "I like that," or "Not right now," but don't count on it. Real listening skills aren't good manners—they're all that stand between you and a cold, watery grave. One false move and the last sounds you hear will be the creaking of the hull and the screams of your crew as the ocean swallows another ship of fools.

✳ We All Live in a Yellow Submarine ✳

What we've just described is tricky to pull off. Most human beings, whether boys or girls, don't have very good listening skills. Even the people who know how to lean back and take in another person's message have their own problem: They don't know how to communicate in return. In fact, you can neatly break the human race down into those who don't know how to listen and those who don't know how to talk. A few genuinely miserable souls can't do either, and wind up expressing themselves with semiautomatic weapons at a nearby McDonald's, but that's a different problem.

So if you find yourself prattling on until your friends' eyes glaze over, it's time to brush up on your listening skills. If, on the other hand, you feel as though no one pays attention, and everyone else is always imposing their ideas on poor little you, it's time to learn how to get your point across without resorting to passive-aggressive maneuvers such as agreeing with everything someone says, and then doing the exact opposite.

But neither good listening nor good speaking will help you if you're a coward about women. If you can't work up the nerve to make first contact—the first *meaningful* contact, not just "hi there"—then no matter how wonderful she might think you are, you'll pass each other like ships in the night.

When you allow this to happen, you are living in a yellow submarine. Your first mate tells you, "There's a ship off the port bow; should we break radio silence?"

"No, no," you say. "She's not really interested in us."

"But, Captain," your mate cries out, "she's signaling with eye contact and semaphore! And she just nibbled on her hair! Shouldn't we let her know we're on the same side?"

"Back to your post, Mister," you tell him sternly. "She probably has a boyfriend already, and even if she doesn't, she couldn't possibly want to talk to us."

And so you dive deep, and later that night you shoot off a torpedo when no one's looking. What you'll never know could fill a library. Was she a cool person? Was she looking at you, or the guy behind you? Is it possible that the two of you had something in common? You yellow bastard, you've condemned your crew to a long, lonely cruise under the Arctic Sea. If they mutiny, don't come crying to us.

So why do boys do this? We've all heard women grind their teeth in exasperation about boys who won't make the first move. Then again, we've heard them go on at insufferable length about boys who *do,* and they seem to be equally insulted and inconvenienced by both, so it's a miracle the species continues to reproduce, but that's a side point which we're not going to get distracted by. The issue that needs attention is why don't you when you *should?*

One word: Insecurity.

You figure you aren't interesting enough *(but she'd know that you are if only she took the time),* handsome enough *(and yet you have a special inner beauty),* rich enough *(but someday soon you will be),* funny enough *(even though your best friends laugh at your jokes sometimes),* smart enough *(although you have some cool areas of expertise),* or well hung enough *(but there was that famous soul song, "It Ain't the Meat, It's the Motion," and maybe it's her favorite).*

All of these reasons are bullshit. They're just a small sample of excuses you give yourself for cowardice. And let's face it, there are always a million reasons *not* to do something. Your authors, for instance, can think of over seventy-five good arguments for not getting out of bed in the morning. Sometimes we even use them, and lie there for days, afraid to write, moaning and cringing whenever the phone rings. In fact, this entire chapter was written by a friend of ours while we hid under our respective blankies, saying we had "the fear."

The message is an old one, but it still applies: The blunders you commit through action are never so deadly as what you miss if you don't act at all. As Julius Caesar said, "Fortune favors the bold." And as Nike tells us, when it paraphrases Zen to sell overpriced shoes made in Malaysian slave-labor camps, "Just do it."

As we said before, you just need to work the qualities that you *do* have. Life is too short to go around trying to be everything to everyone—just look at what that did to Michael Jackson. No, be yourself, and don't worry.

Sure, that's easy enough for us to say. Especially when there are so many things to feel insecure about. Especially if you feel—how shall we put this delicately?—under-endowed. Yes, we can point out that Howard Stern got rich off a diminutive pecker, but he's an exception, right?

Wrong.

Making Peace with Mr. Happy

We boys are kind of strange when it comes to our cocks. This has been discussed a lot; the way we name them, coddle them, speak to them, and generally let them make all our important decisions. If you ever see a stand-up comedian who doesn't have a segment about men and how they think of their dicks, demand your money back. You've been cheated.

What all of this fails to account for is how ambivalent we are about Mr. Happy. There is no such thing as a one-sided coin, and there's no such thing as a loving relationship that doesn't have a flip side of hatred and fear. We all know why, how, and when we love our powerful pillars of penetration. We can murmur sweet nothings about our heat-seeking missiles of love for the next century.

But what about those darker feelings? The time you noticed that it leaned to the left and you thought, *Oh my God, there must be something horribly wrong with me, maybe if I masturbate with my left hand it will go back.* Or the time you were in the high school shower and you realized that you weren't such a big boy after all? Or that you were freakishly large, and everybody kept staring?

Admittedly, the problem of being too big isn't seen as a problem at all by most boys, since we are taught to believe that more is always more. But listen to women talking honestly about sex, and you'll hear them discussing boys who were so large that they couldn't fit in. No matter how you slice it, this is a serious problem. Not one that most of us have any sympathy for, sure, but it still ain't fun to be in bed and have her saying *"Aieeee, stop! Something's tearing!"* instead of "Yeah, oooooh, do it to me more, mm-hmmm."

But all things considered, the li'l guys have it the worst. While it's no longer polite to make fun of someone for being Hispanic, female, gay, or skinny, no one has any problems with making itty-bitty dickie jokes. (Or fat jokes, but we'll get to that in the next chapter.)

First, it's good to remember that women's genitals come in all sizes, too. A snug fit is what you should hope for, not a painful bout of stretch aerobics. If she's too large and you're too small, the dreaded words "Is it in?" may be uttered, and everything will end, not with a bang, but with a whimper. And as we pointed out, if she's underdeveloped and you're overendowed, only pain can result. Unless both of you are into ripped membranes as a sexual fetish, this will be a turnoff.

Second, your mate should be into *you,* not your package. Vibrator manufacturers have advanced to such a point that if our John Thomases needed to be permanently replaced they could be, with guaranteed next-day delivery, and five-year on-site service contracts. So there have to be a wider variety of reasons for women putting up with our antics.

And third, you should consider the story of . . .

✳ The Man with the Itty-Bitty Penis ✳

Tim Bennett (name not changed since we couldn't be bothered) wants to be the banner-bearer for under-hung men everywhere—no matter how diminutive that flag may turn out to be. In the time your authors have known him, he has never had a problem with telling everyone about his eeny-meeney moe. "I have a small penis," he would declaim to shocked friends and co-workers. "But, boy, is it *hard.*"*

We all laughed and attributed his gung-ho attitude to comic ambition. Tim does stand-up work now and then, and as we noted earlier, no comic is considered a professional until he can spend at least a half hour making dick jokes. And anyway, if Tim's wang-diddle were really so wee, would he go around saying so? Nah, odds were that he was really average, and trying to work out a line of patter. Some comics are like that, always experimenting on their friends.

Then Tim began dating a woman who happened to be a really

---

* Actually, the idea of small dicks being cooler than big ones dates back to the ancient Greeks, who believed that a big cock was apt to be soft and spongy. Socrates got in no trouble at all when he promised to make his students' minds strong and their dicks short. However, Socrates was said to be an extremely ugly man, and the Athenians were as beauty-obsessed as a convention of supermodels, so some scholars suggest he was executed for being unsightly. *Not* for shrinking his pupils' dicks.

drop-dead gorgeous *femme fatale.* We'd pull her aside and pepper her with questions. Was he really that small? Come on, he was average to middling, right?

She'd smile her blindingly perfect smile and say, "Oh, I guess he's small." But the way she said it was sort of charming and half-kidding, so we drew our own conclusions. He probably had her in on the joke. Nobody except Howard Stern would go around saying he was small if it were the truth.

Then the engagement was announced, and much to our surprise, they never broke it off. By the time we were realizing that they might actually *mean* it, it was time for the wedding. Stupefied, we were obligated to provide a bachelor party, which entailed us giving a lot of money to a guy we didn't entirely trust, and planning out the most humiliating evening we could imagine.

That's the thing women fail to understand about bachelor parties: They assume it's about providing the groom-to-be with an evening of tawdry sex and titillation. That's for everyone else. The main man, on the other hand, is plied with hard alcohol, slapped repeatedly, stripped of all dignity, and humiliated in front of all his closest friends. Among the more harebrained schemes considered for Tim was knocking him unconscious and leaving him in a flophouse with no clothing, but ample evidence of hard drug use the night before, and an assortment of revealing lingerie.[†] In the end we settled on a standard ritual of abasement, using the time-honored tools, strippers and alcohol.

Since Tim is a professional comic who used to work for Second City, the party consisted of forty or fifty *other* comics, all of whom

---

[†] This was abandoned when some killjoy pointed out that we didn't know if Tim might have an allergic reaction to any of the standard knockout drugs. We tried to obtain his medical records, but failed. We were also a little hazy about what the standard knockout drugs were. Ammonium was suggested, but we're pretty sure that would have just killed him, which wasn't really the point.

were trying to be funny. We won't mention names, but the sight of television comedians and stage comedians trying to be hilarious at the same time is ugly beyond imagination. Brendan was so terrified that he volunteered to tend bar, just so he'd have something between him and all of that humor, while Spitznagel manfully waded into the mess, telling dick jokes as he went. Tim looked sort of dazed, which only got worse as the guests forced cheap tequila and cheaper cigars into his mouth. By the time the strippers arrived, he was half a shot away from terminal alcohol poisoning, stumbling and moaning as various friends slapped his face and pounded on his shoulders.

The strippers set up a boom box and began doing their routine in that tired, bored way that indicates professionalism. The forty or so comics, all of whom would pretend to be world-weary and cynical whenever they thought someone was watching, scooted up to the stage with wide eyes and dangling jaws. You'd think they'd never seen a naked woman before. When the time came for Tim to be worked over by the dancers, several of his most trusted friends pinned him to the floor and ripped off his clothing. The process was made complicated by the fact that everyone was drunk, as well as Tim's unnaturally huge Nike Air cross-training monstrosities. Nobody could figure out how to get them unstrapped, unzipped, unlaced, or whatever the hell you do with those things. But off came the shirt, and the pants were rolled down to bunch up by the Nikes. As his boxer shorts were yanked past his ass by a comedian whose name we won't mention,‡ Tim lurched to his feet. We'll never know if he was trying to escape, but before he was pulled back to the ground, he turned in a circle, looking out at the forty or fifty people who wanted nothing more than to see him disgraced and broken. And as he turned to face us, every man in the room was thinking the same thing:

‡ The check he sent us cleared.

Wow, that's a really small penis.

Tim had not been lying for effect. It was a pinkish nub, a sort of overgrown clitoris, even smaller than the ones you see on those statues of Greek Gods. And in the midst of his torment, Tim had been forced to show it to almost every man he knew. Instead of howling with derisive laughter, the way it would happen in a movie, the crowd seemed embarrassed for him, shamed by his shame. Pouring unnatural amounts of alcohol into him was okay; abusing him physically was part of the program; forcing him into lewd and demeaning acts while he couldn't defend himself was *de rigueur;* but publicly airing his miniature manhood was too goddamn much. We had crossed the line.

Tim, on the other hand, lit up at the sight of our downcast faces. Suddenly he came alive from his drunken stupor and raised his arms into the air in a kind of salute. This was his pale, skinny body, and this was his cock, and he was proud of it all. "Yeah," he screamed, "yeaaaaaah!"

The comics were subdued for the rest of the evening, but something had been released in Tim, and he couldn't get enough. As one of the strippers spanked his ass with an unlikely leather device, he shouted with glee. He refused to pull his pants back up.

A week later we shifted around in hardwood pews, watching him marry one of the most beautiful women we had ever seen. At the end of the ceremony, a female dwarf sang gospel music. Everyone was impressed. Several people wept.

And as we watched the happy couple walk down the aisle, we couldn't help but think that if you grouped Tim with the authors of this book in a slightly modified police lineup, you'd have a representative sample of male members, ranging from small to medium to large. And wasn't it ironic that the smallest of the lot was now happily married, while the Mr. Medium had a steady girlfriend, and the largest was picking up the pieces of several spectacularly failed romances.

Let this be a lesson to boys everywhere. Size may matter, but nobody ever said whether that was big size or little size. It may be shocking, but you need to accept the truth of the matter. Based on what we've seen, less is *definitely* more.

Kinky Sex

or,

"I Love You So Much I Want to Tie You Up with
Chains and Beat You with Warm Squash"

Although there are still a few people who denounce everything except baby-making sex as evil, most of America has cozied up to the idea of kink as a "lifestyle choice." Some of kink's more vocal advocates claim that it is a mainline to the hidden parts of your psyche, a sort of urgent Post-It note from your subconscious. Others take the "lifestyle" part very seriously, and define their entire existence by the unusual sex they practice. All of this is well and good, but it doesn't answer a more basic question: what, exactly, *is* kinky?

The missionary position isn't. Neither is doggie-style, although a few timid souls may think of it with a shudder of shame. Oral sex used to be kinky, but that was before man discovered fire; these days you'd have to put your mouth in some fairly unlikely places before the rest of us would even consider nominating you as a pervert. And same-sex shenanigans aren't nearly so kinky as they used to be, especially with so many stable, domestic gay and lesbian couples throwing sand in the gears of our collective sexual imagination.

So what's left? Bondage? Hell, there are handbooks on the subject, readily available at the bookstore-cum-coffeehouse nearest you. Tasteful, yuppified sex shops sell "Bondage Starter Kits," which double as lovely wedding presents. The overhyped after-school special for the stage, *Rent,* even chants the letters "S and M!" during one of its many forgettable songs. And if you can find us a co-ed who doesn't own a pair of handcuffs, we'll give you a shiny new nickel.

No, if you want to achieve kinkhood, you'll have to go farther afield.* Exactly *how* much farther is up to you, but we'd strongly suggest you avoid crossing the line into something criminal. As sexually exciting as you may find the idea of holding midgets at gunpoint in a basement while you force them to watch porn films and sing "Tie a Yellow Ribbon Round the Old Oak Tree," you'll probably be arrested if you try it. On the other hand, there's nothing wrong with *persuading* them to do it—indeed, if you can talk two or three dwarfs into helping you act out your fantasy, you're well on your way to being a card-carrying pervert.

One thing to remember is that any discussion of kink is incomplete. There are so many fetishes, so many subtle perversions that no author can hope to catalog them all. A brief stop in an adult bookstore will drive this point home—who would have thought, for instance, that there would be enough of a market to support an entire magazine devoted to tickling the feet of women dressed as cowboys? And if this is volume eight, what were the first seven issues like? Meaning to say, that's a *really* specific kink. And yet, if experience is any guide, people get minute and particular about what gets their crankcase turning.

Bearing this in mind, we're going to give you a quick (and incomplete) run-down of some practices which you may or may not want to bring to bed.

---

* And if you live in San Francisco, you're completely out of luck, since its residents view almost everything as a "lifestyle choice," which pisses us off to no end. If we're caught frolicking naked in the park with a greased sheep, we want it to be *wrong*. What's the point of being a pervert if everyone's brimming with tolerance and understanding? *Non sequitur:* it does not follow.

S/M

This is one of the most popular forms of kink—indeed, so common that it stands to lose its perverse standing if someone doesn't condemn it loudly, publicly, and soon. There are a bunch of variants that fall into this category, ranging from the banal (bondage) to the hardcore (master-slave relationships). What all thirty-six flavors of S/M have in common is a simple concept, which is often lost in the whips, spreader bars, fleece-lined cuffs, and the ever-multiplying knickknacks of leather life:

You don't want to, I make you, you like it.

That's all you'll ever need to know. Sure, it gets dressed up in fancy toys and rhetoric, but almost all S/M boils down to this simple equation. Although it is customary to dominate a partner with old-fashioned things like spankings and nipple clips, there's really no reason you couldn't accomplish the same thing with licorice and a Slinky. So long as someone resists, someone else pushes the issue, and everybody has an orgasm, you're on the right track.

If you're interested in being the dominated partner in this sort of relationship, you're in for a bit of a hunt. According the people who practice S/M, dominants are far less numerous than submissives. This seems odd and counterintuitive, until you consider the couchpotato mentality of America. Tying someone up and spanking their ass until they beg for Daddy takes *effort*. People who enjoy inflicting controlled pseudo-violence can get much better-paying work at any video game design company, not to mention the World Wrestling Federation. Why should they give it to you for free, eh?

Voyeurism/Exposurism

Public sex will always have a place in our hearts. Whether it's sweater-groping in a car on lover's lane, or keeping the curtains up in the bedroom, Americans aren't very stuck-up about a little flash-

ing. There are, of course, matters of degree. Going without underwear will get almost no one in trouble, even in the more extreme
cases involving large dance clubs and short skirts. On the other
hand, anything involving a trench coat and a schoolgirl will cause
problems, and we must gently discourage this sort of thing.

But before you get moody, we should go back to our example
with midgets and porn films. Part of the fun of
kinky sex is that you use your *imagination*. Just
because something illegal and distasteful gets
you hot doesn't mean you have to do it—why
not, for instance, play out a filthy flashing fantasy with your girlfriend? And if the schoolgirl
element is vital to your kicks, you can always
have her dress like one. *Voilà!* In the privacy of
your own home you can now play out your illegal fantasy to your heart's content, and never involve the police. Unless, that is, you want your
girlfriend to dress like a cop and arrest you, but
that's role-playing, and we'll get to that later.

Group sex

The idea of this is that a whole lot of sweaty, naked bodies are inherently more fun than just a couple of sweaty, naked bodies. This
may be true, but you will run into some difficulties. You ought to
invite an even number of people, for obvious reasons. Also, it's hard
enough to find one woman who's attractive and compatible in bed,
so how much *more* difficult is it to find a large group of people with
whom you wouldn't mind grunting? And exactly how many people
do you want to have seeing your flabby ass naked, anyway?

Swinging

Swinging is group sex, only more selective. You and your partner pick another couple, and the two groups play a spirited bout of mix'n'match. We approve of swinging much more than generalized group sex, since everyone is more likely to get personalized attention. Also, swinging is more patriotic. Orgies were perfected in Rome, whereas swinging reached its apex in the good old U.S. of A. If you're going to be kinky, you might as well do it with pride in America.

Sex toys

There aren't many good sex toys for boys, but there are some lovely gadgets you can bring to bed. Encouraging your sweetheart to play with a vibrator while you do the nasty can lead to all sorts of athletic and aesthetic surprises. We know some boys quail at this thought, fearing that their honey will like the plastic toy better than the fleshly one. But as we pointed out earlier in this chapter, if women really wanted to permanently replace our packages, they could, and FedEx would lead the charge.

Your opportunities for toys expand if you're playing with bondage. Indeed, the tools and accessories of bondage are so numerous and costly that your authors have come to believe that outfitting a child for hockey season is cheaper by half. But if you've got the dough, there are plenty of goodies to be had.

Rough sex

We aren't talking about a little scratching here. We're talking about balls-to-the-wall sex, with lots of biting and tumbling, and maybe some broken furniture. There's nothing like demolishing a bedroom to let you know you had a good night.

We'd write more on the subject, but we're still sore, and the marks aren't fading as quickly as we'd like.

Role-playing

In some ways, role-playing is kink at its most primal. Whether you're playing a modified version of Cowboys and Indians, or a hearty game of Master and Servant, role-playing draws on skills you learned in the sandbox. Indeed, many kinks would be impossible to practice without this primal tool. While it's terribly risky to have sex with a complete stranger, it's kinda fun to *pretend* you and your girl have just met, and go from there.

The ravishment fantasy, which is far more common than we'd like, would be a terrible burden to mankind if not for role-playing. One woman summarized it by saying, "Harrison Ford's at your door, and he won't take 'no' for an answer." Imagine, if you will, an entire nation of women waiting for Harrison to beat down their doors and take them by force. The mind boggles. But with role-playing, you and your lady love can act out the most edgy fantasies imaginable, without risking a lifetime of maximum security correctional facilities.

Phone sex

There's something inherently silly about phone sex, but that doesn't stop us from loving it. In many ways it's the purest form of role-playing, since all you've got are words and noises, and everything interesting goes on between your ears. Although some people are willing to pay for it, you'll be happiest if you do your heavy breathing with someone you know.

The only exception to this rule is the dreaded long-distance relationship. Once you're done pouring your heart out to your baby, you shouldn't go further and get into phone sex, since by the time you're both finished you'll have a bigger phone bill than if you'd called 1-900-HOT-MAMA in the first place.

Cross-dressing, cybersex, fun with ice, tickling, etc.

As we said before, any list of kinks is incomplete. We could go on forever and still not list the stuff you're into. But a massive resource awaits you, a never-ending expanse of titillation and excitement, a world of untapped potential and joy. It will be there for you when no one else can be. It will open up your mind to new and exciting sexual practices. It will force you to go through the beaded curtain at the back of the video store. We are talking, of course, about commercial pornography.

Porn

Whether it's magazines, videos or late-night cable, men have always been suckers for good old-fashioned American porn. As the late U.S. Supreme Court Justice Potter Stewart once noted, "I know obscenity when I see it." You got that right, Stewie. And that's exactly why we love porn so much. There's no doubting that it's obscene. Men are visual creatures and porn provides us with plenty of ocular filth to feast our eyes on.

But porn isn't just a man's best friend. In some ways, it defines manhood. Sure, it's shocking and explicit and in bad taste, but isn't that exactly what male sexuality is all about? In real life, we're supposed to be polite boys who treat our partners with respect and sensitivity. But porn gives us a chance to let our true sexual identities shine. We're allowed to hoot and holler, let our guts hang out, beat our chests, and make complete asses of ourselves. No self-respecting woman would ever let us get away with that in real life, and we wouldn't expect them to. As long as porn is there to let us wallow in the sheer stupidity of our sexual instincts and get it out of our systems, we're happy campers.

But it's becoming more difficult to find good porn these days. Thanks to the rise of "art-house" porn, adult video sections are being flooded with selections that confuse and alarm the tradition-bound porn hound. These films typically consist of heavily choreographed sex scenes, performed by well-cut models and lit in romantic, bluish mood-lighting. As any old-fashioned smut-loving guy could tell you, there's more to porn than explicit shots of sex. And proper porn certainly has nothing to do with beautiful people having perfect sex under fluorescent light as New Age music plays in the background. That, if anything, is porn *lite,* one concealed penis away from a perfume ad. It's the type of pseudo-erotica that Neo-Yuppies and feminists are so fond of, graphic enough to make them feel naughty but still sanitized and glossy so as not to offend their genteel genitalia.

The first-time porn consumer may be unaware of what to look for, and is less likely to know the difference between an actual porn video and something that would be more appropriate at an experimental film festival. As a service to those readers who honestly want to be able to identify real porn when they see it, we have put together a short primer course in porn aesthetics.

a) Bad plot
(or "But I Didn't Order Any Pizza!")

Conventional wisdom has it that porn fans fast forward through the plots to get to the sex scenes. This is not true. In fact, we more often fast forward through the *sex* to get back to the *plot*. Porn videos have plots that are so absurd and preposterous that they tend to be more exciting than the sex itself.

Let's face it, there are only so many opportunities for sex in real life. But in porn, any situation you might find yourself in can, and probably will, result in an exchange of bodily fluids. You order pizza and end up screwing the delivery guy. You invite over some friends and it turns into an orgy. You call a plumber and  he tells you which pipes he *really* wants to inspect. In the porno universe, anybody is a potential sex partner: Your boss, the landlord, a policeman, a drifter and—our personal favorite—a three-headed alien who needs "man seed" as fuel to get back to her planet.

b) Ugly actors (or "Are Those Sagging Tits or
Are You Just Happy to See Me?")

There's a very good reason why porn actors are not very attractive; it makes the typical porn consumer feel better about his own sexual inadequacies. Most of us don't look good naked, and we look even worse having sex. We don't want to watch beautiful people having athletic sex in a manner that we couldn't possibly compete with even after years of practice. We want to look at overweight and balding men having clumsy sex with trailer park trash bimbos with big hair, duotone-creme-finish fake fingernails, and pimples on their butts.

The most popular porn actors are essentially evolutionary misfits, low on the food chain, mammals-in-theory. They include guys like Rick Savage, whose unibrow and propensity for mouth-breathing and spittle make even the most unattractive leading lady shudder. And John Leslie, with his constant sneer, bloodshot eyes, and wheezy muttering, who is so goddamn creepy that you'd swear he has some rotting corpses stashed behind the walls of his home. And, of course, there is Ron "The Hedgehog" Jeremy, the *crème de la crème.* This man has it all: the tremendous potbelly, the white man's Afro, the sniggering wit, the ape-like body hair, and a penis the size of Florida. He is foul on so many levels that you cannot help but cheer him on.

Then there are the actresses, a group of uninhibited hussies who represent the heart and soul of porn. All porn starlets, from classy bimbos like Seka and Marilyn "Ivory Soap" Chambers to contemporary whores-for-hire like Amber Lynn and Ashlyn Gere, have one thing in common: they have absolutely no redeeming qualities whatsoever. Physically, they're a mess. Their bodies are covered with bruises, moles, acne, cesarean scars, needle marks, unidentifiable lesions, and tattoos in inappropriate places. Their personalities aren't much better. They hardly ever talk, limiting their dialogue to four key phrases: "It's so big," "Give it to me now," "Yeah, baby, yeah," and "I want more." When not speaking (which is often) they bide their time by staring blankly into space and making yelps of pleasure that sound eerily like a baby seal being clubbed to death.

But there is something undeniably lovable about porn hags. They're so earnest about their work, so convinced that they're involved in a reputable craft, that you end up taking them as seriously as they do. Before long you'll find yourself following their careers, noticing the subtle complexities of their characters, and debating with your friends, without sarcasm, their "blond" period versus their "brunette" period.

c) Other clues

TACKY SETTINGS: If it doesn't look as if it was filmed in some guy's garage or one-bedroom apartment, then it probably isn't porn. The majority of porn settings contain the following: a sofa and/or bed, a dead plant on a rickety end table, and a framed poster of a Budweiser model on the wall. Anything else is unnecessary, or if it is included, must be essential to setting the scene. (For example, bars on the window indicate that we are in a prison, a lava lamp indicates that we are on another planet, etc.) In the rare occasion when the action takes place in an exotic location, it will most likely be in the backyard of the director's home. But outdoor settings are hardly ever used because porn actors fear sunlight.

THE "MONEY SHOT": Also known as the "pop shot," this is the Grand Finale by which the porn stud earns his paycheck. The male ejaculation is visible in shocking detail, so clinically exposed that you will often feel like you're witnessing some sort of twisted science experiment. But we are not only treated to the horrifying spectacle of sperm exiting the penis, we also watch as it covers everything in its path: the bed, the lamp, the ceiling, a car parked outside. Nothing is safe from the onslaught of this foul discharge. In the world of porn, the ability to emit gallons of semen from your body is the only true sign of masculinity.

SYNTH-ROCK SOUND TRACK: The typical porn sound track is a weird amalgam of watered-down funk and Barry White Muzak, all performed by a tinny synthesizer. Apparently we are to believe that every porn stud has the same lame taste in music. But the porn sound track does more than cover up the painfully overacted moans of pleasure. It is also used as an aphrodisiac of sorts. In the porn milieu, all a horny stud need do to get his lady in the mood is play a little synth-rock on the hi-fi and *boom,* she's good to go. Amazing as it sounds, casiotone has actually replaced foreplay!

SEVENTIES OR EARLY EIGHTIES FASHION: Porn actors seem to be trapped in a time warp in which the fashion of the seventies never went out of style. The men dress in bell-bottoms, gold chains, and flowery shirts unbuttoned to the navel. They wax their mustaches, grow their sideburns to their chins, and never take off their tube socks, wearing them like a badge of honor. The women have huge hair that would be laughable even on an episode of *Charlie's Angels,* and wear such heavy makeup that it would be easy to mistake them for a member of a Kiss tribute band. With the latest crop of straight-to-video smut boxes, porn-makers have tried to update the classic seventies look, with results that are even more horrifying. The men sport blow-dried hair that would look excessive on Duran Duran, and sometimes wear headbands instead of tube socks. The women have more piercings, and their big hair contains the occasional streak of color. There is absolutely no irony in any of these fashion choices, as no one in porn has a sense of humor.

POOR VIDEO QUALITY: Porn is always shot on the lowest-grade video available, so don't bother messing with the tracking on your TV. The actors' skin looks orange, the room looks pinkish-green, and the picture is either foggy and out-of-focus or painfully sharp and jaggy. But this is no accident—it is a stylistic choice. Porn directors have spent over twenty years perfecting the inferior look of their videos. It is one of the most time-honored traditions of porn.

DÉJÀ VU: If one of the actors looks familiar to you, if you swear that you'd seen him or her before on an old episode of *Xena: Warrior Princess* or a John Waters movie, or maybe they look like someone you used to date in high school but their breasts weren't as big back then, then you are probably watching porn.

TITLES: The next time you're at your local video store and you're in the mood for really great porn, don't look at the models on the boxes. Instead, examine the titles. *Night Whispers* is probably just another plotless celebration of attractive people fulfilling each other's needs. But *D-Cup Robot Bitch Queens, Part III: Anal Armageddon . . .* now *that* has potential.

Of course, being able to differentiate between wanna-be smut and true filth takes years of training, and doing it from titles alone may be impossible for the beginner. This problem worried our editor, Bruce Tracy, so much that he sent us a very strange document. He had been writing down the titles of porn triple-features that were playing at a local adult cinema. The features changed every week. A quick scan of the file and some kitchen math showed that he had been doing this for well over two years.

His explanation for this obsessive-compulsive behavior was that he found the titles "creatively weird." Suuuure you did, Bruce. And when we buy triple-packs of *Spanking Nun Monthly* from the seedy adult bookshop on the corner, it's just our form of, um, social research.

But we're not here to speculate on the sexual obsessions of our editor, whose door is often closed at odd hours, and who, to the best of our knowledge, never paid over two grand to the Singh Travel and Leisure Service for a sex tour of Thailand. No, all we're going to do is pass some highlights on to you. Study it carefully. See if you can find what these titles have in common, for this may be an important clue. And while you're at it, reflect on the sort of man who would take the time to record porn titles for two years.

Hot Craving Mouth	Hot Voluptuous Girls
Hot Hungry Mouth	Hot Bad Girls
Hot Luscious Lips	Hot Valley Girls
Hot Juicy Whoppers	Hot Body Invasion
Hot Bodacious Boobs	Hot French Lesson
Hot Juicy Buns	Hot Driving Desires
Hot Tempting Buns	Hot Dragon Lady
Hot Sizzling Buns	Hot Southern Romp
Hot Blazing Tails	Hot Sizzling Coven
Hot Anal Maniac	Hot Blond Bimbo
Hot Anal Arsenal	Hot Dirty Shame
Hot Anal Webb	Hot Sex Maniac
Hot Backdoor Treat	Hot Sex Challenge
Hot Backdoor Entry	Hot Sexual Fantasy
Hot Oriental Orgy	Hot Sexual Slaves
Hot Intimate Orgy	Hot Sizzling Debut
Hot Sexual Orgy	Hot Private Diary
Hot Sultry Nurses	Hot Latex Sex
Hot Horny Nurses	Hot and Bedazzled
Hot Busty Nurses	Hot Haunted Nights
Hot Pleasure Dome	Hot New Positions

Hot Gang Bangers

Hot Girls Fantasy

Hot Dark Alley

Hot Candy Factory

Hot Sex Academy

Hot Loving

Hot Miss Liberty

Hot Intimate Affairs

Hot Sultry Ways

Hot Girls Fantasy

Handle with Care:
Contents May Be Broken

(Understanding the
Modern Woman)

Scenario:

*The two of you wound up back at your place, and it's been every-
thing you could have hoped for. Maybe you're already having sex,
though that's too clinical a term for the passionate gymnastics taking
place on your bed. Maybe you're on top, or maybe she's riding you for
all you're worth, but who cares? It's good either way. You're both going crazy with fingers and tongues, and it's rising to a crescendo, moving toward that perfect moment when you'll both convulse in ecstasy,
unified in a final, holy apex of pleasure, and it's so good, so right . . .*

*And then it stops. For a moment you're confused—is this an elab-
orate tease? One of those tantric sex things where you come close but
don't quite? No, that can't be it. Something's wrong. Next thing you
know, she's out of the bed, dashing for the bathroom, muttering something that sounds suspiciously like, "Dirty . . . oh, so dirty . . ." You
lie there, too stunned to say anything. Faucets run. Toilets flush.*

Then you hear the shower sputtering to life. Stripping the condom from your now-useless member, you rise and approach the bathroom door, knocking lightly.

"Are you okay?"

"Just fine," she calls out in a quavering voice. "Everything's fine!"

You stand there, dumbfounded. What went wrong? Was it something you did? Something you said? You hear a lot of splashing in there—just how hard is she scrubbing? Over the spray you hear ragged breathing, as though she were suppressing tears. "I'm clean, Mommy," she cries out suddenly, "I'm clean!"

And whether you know it or not, you've just had a run-in with Women's Issues. What's worse, you got off lightly.

Okay, so maybe it didn't happen like that. Instead, you mentioned Scotland over lunch, and she suddenly stopped talking. For a week. Or perhaps you don't even know what triggered the freak-out, which makes you even more edgy and desperate. It could happen again, at any time, for reasons unknown.

Confused? Upset? Angry? Go ahead, let it out. We're all in the same boat on this one. Women's Issues are enough to make a strong man run screaming into the night. The unavoidable problem is that once you've entered her body, you're going to enter her life, and, more importantly, her mind. Here be monsters, brave wanderer—here be demons.

Of course, men are fed a whole lot of bullshit about love, sex, and dating, and before you go pointing it out, we know that men have their touchy subjects, too. But here's the thing of it: Women's issues are completely different from ours, since they have been fed a divergent set of lies from birth. All of the wrongheaded advice we boys have already digested and shat out is nothing, *nothing* compared to the damage done to young girls by illustrated books about dolphins and unicorns. When you think about the contradictory signals they're given about love and dating, from "Sex is beautiful" to "Don't touch your dirty place," it's a wonder they don't walk around with nonstop nosebleeds.

You don't have to be sucked under by the complexity, but you should get on your knees and thank Jah the Great Spirit you didn't have to handle the hard stuff. It's probable that she worked out the vast majority of the bullshit by the time she turned twenty. Then again, it's also possible that she didn't, so exercise extreme caution around any woman who has a picture of a unicorn in her room. If it's framed, run for your life.

There seems to be no way for a man to understand a woman's issues. There also seems to be no way to avoid them, unless you luck out and date a completely balanced, healthy individual, in which case the rest of us hate your guts, and we hope she dumps you. For most of us, peeling open the psyche of our beloved is a frightening, messy business. As we piece together the evidence, based on her actions, her words, and her sleep disorders, we start to form a model that looks something like this:

$$\prod_{slut}^{virgin} \triangleright\ ^{purity}\sqrt{Satan} \geq penis\ \downarrow\ _{empowerment}$$

$$\left\{ goddess \overset{ego}{\underset{id}{\sum}} daddy \right\}\ \underset{puberty}{\longleftrightarrow}\ bad\ touch$$

$$\oint\ \succ\ abuse < \overset{victim}{\underset{survivor}{\int}}\ \Longrightarrow 2\ \text{A.M.}\ ^{food}/_{weight}$$

$$_{leather}$$

And in all likelihood, that's an oversimplification. So what are you supposed to do? Play amateur shrink? Put a bag over your head and hope it goes away? Reproduce asexually?

Nobody really knows. The best you can do is master some of the basics, and wing it from there. A good grounding in the classics will help you somewhat, but we're not talking about the *Iliad* or Socrates. There is a distinct body of storytelling by, for, and about women, ranging from the poems of Sappho to *Little Women* to "Dr. Quinn, Medicine Woman." Dismiss it all as chick art at your own risk. There are some important clues into the female psyche buried in these works, stuff that might be useful, even practical. Remember the immortal words of Sun Tzu: "Know your opponent." We're not suggesting that you're out to vanquish your true love—that would be tasteless—but wouldn't it be nice to get a grip on her social conditioning? Wouldn't that give you a bit of an edge the next time she freaks out?

Damn straight it would. And because we're nice guys, we're not even going to suggest that you make a project of reading all of those books and seeing the films. We've boiled the canon down to its essentials, to the few works that fully represent all that is wrongheaded, contradictory, evil, and perniciously pumped into the brains of young girls over extended periods of time.

Study the list carefully, and should the spirit move you, check out the originals. If, after reading and watching these four stories, you still don't understand why some women have relationship issues, well, maybe you should be writing stories about unicorns.

TITLE	PLOT	MESSAGE
Wuthering Heights	Girl and boy share forbidden love, which drives boy over the edge and makes him evil and abusive, except that he's not, except that he is.	Brooding, passionate men are allowed to hit women, so long as you know he really loves you.
The Story of O	Boy loves girl. Girl finds purpose in life through being submissive at an exclusive S/M club. Boy is so thrilled he gives her to an older boy.	You must change yourself radically to please your man, and even then you'll probably get traded.
Gone With the Wind (film version)	Boy finds girl. Boy loses girl when Atlanta burns down. Girl retrieves boy, who winds up leaving anyway because she's such a bitch.	Being mean is a lot of fun, but you lose your man, which was the whole point in the first place.
The Little Mermaid (Disney version)	Girl finds boy, then loses him to girl with bigger tits, then wins him back when she reveals that the other girl is fat. To marry boy, she must stop being a mermaid forever.	If you change yourself completely, abandon your family, and your competition is overweight, you might get your man.

Reigning Cats and Dogs

There is, of course, a darker fear that lurks on the edges of our minds when we consider Women's Issues: What if they're *not* the product of social conditioning? After all, neurologists have discovered differ-ences in how men and women use their brains. And when you con-sider that neurology is a rough, primitive science—they're still at the poke-it-and-see-what-it-does phase—it's quite possible that someone's going to find that men and women are hard-wired *com-pletely* differently. We can only speculate at what sort of ruckus this will cause.

Brendan raised this fear with his older brother, Jim, since he is more practical and sensible than Brendan can ever hope to be. Also, Jim has successfully lived with a woman for thirteen or fourteen years, which beats the best records by your authors all to hell.

"I don't know how we're going to tackle Women's Issues," Bren-dan groaned over lunch. "We have to talk about it—I mean, it's a frigging book on dating, so we have no choice. But how are we go-ing to do it without offending everyone?"

Jim nodded. "I know what you mean. For instance, I've been vol-unteering a lot of my time at an animal shelter."

Brendan looked at his brother quizzically.

"No, really, this relates back to what you were saying. So after a week of cleaning cages and helping show animals to the families that come to adopt, I noticed that all of the cats were female. All of them. Care to guess why?"

"I dunno," Brendan said, frowning. "Maybe people are more bru-tal with males? Kill 'em instead of throw them out?"

Jim shook his head.

"Okay," Brendan said, his mind a blank, "this is weird. Do male cats have shorter life spans or something like that? Like, they're more likely to catch a fatal disease on the street?"

"Nope," Jim said. "Wrong again."

"Well screw me, I don't have the foggiest. Why?"

Jim smiled. "It took me a while to figure it out, but it's like this: The males tend to be more outgoing and friendly; they come right up and nuzzle your hand; they're playful. They get adopted like *that,*" he said, snapping his fingers. "As soon as they're in the shelter, they're out again. But the females we get are moody. They're more likely to scratch. So they don't get adopted, and we wind up caging and feeding them pretty much forever."

Brendan considered this for a moment. Then the ramifications of what his brother was saying hit home. "Holy shit," he breathed, "I can't print that. That's the most offensive, dangerous thing I've ever heard. You're saying there's some kinda biological mechanism that makes the males friendly and the females touchy."

"I'm just saying what I see," Jim responded levelly.

"Bro, I can't possibly put that in the book."

"Well, whatever you do, don't attach my name to it. My girlfriend would kill me. She's touchy about these things," Jim said.

There's No Hatred Like Self-Hatred (Like No Hatred I Know) *or,* "Honey, Does This Dress Make My Ass Look Fat?"

Just in case you're really stupid and you haven't noticed, we'll say it in words of one syllable: Chicks are strange when it comes to weight. No matter how skeletal they become, they always seem to believe they must lose more, eat less, exercise harder. Admittedly, some women are sane about their bodies, but for most the fat issue is as pressing and strange as the penis size issue is for boys. They obsess about it on a scale that defies our imagination. Trying to wrap our brains around this problem, we called up the Council on Size and Weight

Discrimination.* The woman we reached quoted us the following figures:

- Young girls are more afraid of becoming fat than they are of nuclear war, cancer, or losing their parents.

- Fifty percent of nine-year-old girls and eighty percent of ten-year-old girls have dieted.

- The average American woman is five foot four inches tall, weighs 140 pounds, and wears a size fourteen dress.

- Fifty percent of American women are on a diet at any one time.

- Two thirds of dieters regain the weight lost within one year. Virtually all regain it within five years.

- The diet industry (foods, programs, drugs, etc.) rakes in more than forty billion dollars each year.

- Anorexia has the highest mortality rate (up to 20 percent) of any psychiatric diagnosis.

Now, even if the council's numbers are cooked,† those are some freaky figures. As boys, we've always known women were strange about weight. We just never knew *how* strange.

---

* Which was exactly what it sounds like. The council, which we suspect is one or two people in a shed with a phone and a photocopier, can be reached at P.O. Box 305, Mount Marion, N.Y. (914) 679-1209.

† And we have every reason to suspect they are—come on, anorexia kills people more often than paranoid psychosis? Get real. For every woman dead from under-eating, we're willing to bet there are six postal workers who got whacked by a co-worker who beheld a 600-foot-tall burning marmoset that told him, "Kill them all, before they squander the planet's sand supply."

So what does this mean for you? First of all, walk lightly when it comes to how she looks. Do not *ever* say anything critical about her weight or physical condition. For the average woman, a comment like "That outfit makes you look a little heavy" has the same effect as if she pointed at your male member and told you it reminded her of a garden gnome, only less threatening. No matter how constructive you may think your criticisms may be, keep a lid on it. Allow us to illustrate the correct method:

SHE ASKS . . .	YOU SHOULD SAY . . .
"Does this dress look good on me?"	"Yes. It looks wonderful."
"But you think my butt's getting bigger?"	"I do not, but how could I tell, blinded as I am by your beauty? My lust mounts to untold heights as I gaze upon your perfection."
"You're just saying that to make me feel better."	"No, never! I quake with passion and tremble with longing for your slightest caress! You shine like a living goddess, you shimmer like the stars in heaven; lo, I am the most blest of men that I may behold you!"
"So what's your least favorite part of me?"	"Umm . . . well . . . uhh . . . this is a trick question, right?"
"I knew it! I knew it! You hate my butt!"	*Long groan.*

As should be obvious, there is nothing you can do to help your girlfriend with her body image. All you can hope to do is not make things worse. Physical self-hatred is taught to American women from birth onward, and you don't have a prayer if you try to stand in the way.

Besides, if your woman really *is* large, she has already been subjected to the cruelest degradation anyone can experience without joining a freak show. Mocking fat people is an expression of the last safe prejudice. A person who would never dream of commenting rudely on another's economic condition or skin color feels perfectly safe poking a finger in the stomach of a fat person, chuckling that he needs to lose a few pounds. Frankly, we're surprised that there hasn't been an armed revolt.

And in fairness, taunting overweight people isn't the *only* safe prejudice in America. We're the first to admit that it's also fine in polite society to lump every Muslim into the same terrorist cliché. And in Southern California it's still fashionable to despise immigrants. But fat people have it pretty bad. For every wild-eyed Islamic Fundamentalist you see in the media, there must be at least thirty silly, incompetent fatties. And for every goofy overweight person you see, there must be a hundred ultrathin actors and models shoved in your face.

The media's portrayal of body types is weird and unnatural, and it's not gonna change anytime soon. For whatever reason, our society has decided that an emaciated woman is an attractive woman. There are some nonprofit groups trying to fight this prejudice, including the Council on Size and Weight Discrimination, but it's hard to take these groups seriously when they have names such as Ample Awakenings, FLAB—Fat Lesbian Action Brigade, National Association to Advance Fat Acceptance, People of Size Social Club, and WOW! Women of Width. And lest we forget, Canada hosts a group called PAL, People at Large.

The real problem is that three hundred such

groups as these don't have the impact of a single issue of *Cosmo*. When you get down to brass tacks, nobody stands to make a buck at telling people that they're just fine the way  they are, so advertising agencies (and the companies that hire them) will keep pounding away at women's body image until . . . well, until that day in the hazy future when it ceases to be profitable. In case you were wondering, this is one of those hidden benefits of a market economy. And in more ominous news, some corporations are realizing that money can be made by making *us* feel insecure about our bodies.

Brace yourselves, boys, because over the next few years we're going to be subject to the assault that used to be reserved for women and gay men. More and more advertisements are already featuring perfect, well-built boy toys. If this tactic sells product, expect to see it everywhere. In time we may be as self-hating and self-obsessed about our bodies as women ever were. There may come a day when you turn around and around as you look at yourself in the mirror, and finally ask in exasperation, "Honey, do these jeans make my ass look fat?"

We can only hope that women will handle the answer more tactfully than we usually do.

Your Cheatin' Heart

Why Shouldn't I Screw Around?

Even if you aren't feeling 100 percent sure about the girl you're seeing (and when is anyone?), you shouldn't go playing around. Try to think of the women in your life as big, mean sharks. Once you've reeled one in, it's going to thrash around on the deck of your boat. It'll bite anything that gets near it. This ain't no cute little angelfish on the planks—this is a man-eater that will rip the leg off your cabin boy if he wanders too close. The very *last* thing you should do is go fishing for another one while that monster is bucking around and snapping its jaws. You saw *Jaws* on cable, right? Just think if there'd been a second one in the water.

Hmm, so you aren't convinced? Okay, the shark thing doesn't really fit. Meaning to say, when's the last time someone found a bicycle wheel and a severed hand in the stomach of a girl? No, wait, don't answer that one.

How about a catchy slogan? Would you go for it if we said, "Just say no" a lot? Or maybe we could take a couple of eggs and say, "These are your balls," then smash them with a ball-peen hammer into a hot frying pan, let 'em sizzle, and say, in our most stentorian tone, "These are your balls when your girlfriend finds out you've been fucking around." We could do it just like those no-tolerance, don't-jump-without-a-parachute condom ads, with lots of talk about how you should never-ever-ever do it, no matter how drunk you are, no matter how good that girl over at the end of the bar looks, even though she's giving you the eye, and she's got nipples just like Hershey's Kisses and they're poking through her sweater and her eyes have this kind of mischievous twinkle that suggests maybe she's into some kinky stuff and I mean who knows it couldn't possibly hurt to just talk to her and she's really friendly and kinda sassy and her leg's bumping mine and there's no way anyone here would recognize me from the office or anything like that and she's laughing at my dumb joke and wait a minute her hand's on mine and okay that was just a little kiss not a big kiss you know just a friendly little peck and she gave me her number so who would it hurt if I called her tomorrow I mean it's not like I'm married to my girl and besides it would just be a friendly call and hey everybody likes to make new friends . . .

And Once I've Cheated on Her?

Lie as though your life depended on it, since it does. See if you can minimize the relationship with the new woman, and maybe pretend the whole thing was a one-nighter. Whatever you do, don't tell your girlfriend. For all that she may talk about "wanting to know," trust us on this one, she doesn't. The "I would want to know" line is a coded way of saying, "I need early warning in case I need to rip your still-beating heart from your chest and eat it before your dying eyes."

And What Do I Do After I've Done It a Whole Bunch of Times?

Stop. Don't call the other woman anymore. Just walk away, and maybe you'll escape without serious damage. Try to exercise something resembling self-control. Please. For the children, try.

And When I Keep Doing It Anyway?

Lie a whole lot. Tell big, fat, entertaining whoppers. You're doomed, so there's no reason not to make things worse. Eventually someone's gonna twig to your bedroom antics, and then all hell will break loose, and there won't be a goddamn thing you can do.

What Do I Do When All Hell Breaks Loose?

Change your name. Move to a different state. Enroll in the Federal Witness Protection Program. If things get really bad, check the classifieds to see if there are any job openings in Honduras. You're gonna have two, count 'em, *two* angry women who want to see you suffer. They won't want you dead, oh no, nothing clean and honorable like a knife in the chest or a bullet in the back of the head. Don't expect any Mafioso tactics at this point—an angry woman makes Don Corleone look like Cuddles the Clown.

Can I Make Amends?

No.

Can I Repair My Ruined Reputation?

No.

Can I Win One of the Women Back?

No.

Well What the Hell Do I Do Now, Huh? I Mean, I Was Only Having Some Fun, a Little Something on the Side, and Now Everything's Gone to Shit.

There is nothing you can do.

You Mean I Just Have to Scratch All of the Time and Energy I Put into My Girlfriend Just Because I . . . You Know, Because I Did What I Did?

That is correct.

Come on, I'm a Guy, and Everybody Knows Guys Screw Around Sometimes. It's Natural, Right?

You have half a point there. Behavioral psychologists have established that men want to spurt their seed in as many holes as possible, and that monogamy is not entirely natural. However, before you go thumping your chest and declaring that a harem is your genetic destiny, we must point out that just because an impulse is hard-wired into your genes *does not* mean you have a right to act on it. It's also perfectly natural to hate and kill people who look different from you. So if you're going to argue that cheating is inevitable, you're going to have to accept ethnic cleansing and race riots as inevitable. Face it, spud, not every impulse should be acted upon, no matter how "natural." It's a little concept we call civilization.

Don't Get All Snotty at Me! You Think You're Such a Goddamn Authority Just Because You Have Your Own Book. But I Could Kick Your Ass. Yeah, You Heard Me, I Could Take That Pointy Little Head of Yours and Smack It Till Your Own Mama Don't Know You!

If we understand your question correctly, you're eager to know how to deal with the anger and resentment you'll feel after being dumped by two women. And there's no getting around it; this will be a hard time. We recommend heavy drinking and punching the walls a lot.

What, Didn't You Hear Me, Pipsqueak? Huh? Come on, Put 'Em Up! Lessee What You Got!

Yes, quite correct, you will feel hostility after they've left you, but you can take comfort in knowing it's all your fault.

Hey, Come on, Why Aren't You Scared?

First of all, this is just a book. Second, you've already paid for it. Last, you screwed around on your girl and got caught, so while we can sympathize and we know it must hurt, we can't help laughing at you. There, there. Let it out. Even big boys cry sometimes.

Oh God Oh God, She's Gone. I Can't Believe She's Gone. We Had So Many Good Times—Really Good Times, Man. And Now She's Gone.

Hey, buddy, we're here for ya. Everything's gonna be okay. Come on, cheer up. It ain't so bad.

Yes It Is. Awaaaagh! Oh Man, I Loved Her So Much, I can't Believe It's Over . . . It Can't Be Over . . .

There, there. Take it easy, buddy. Things will get better.

Really? You Mean That? You Think It'll Get Better?

No. We were just saying that to be nice.

The Thin Line Between Love and Hate

(Fights and Breaking Up)

An inevitable part of the dating experience is fighting. No matter how flawless your performance may be, there will come a time when you'll slip up and do something that makes her angry. And then all hell will break loose. If you aren't already terrified of your first fight with a woman, you should be. We are helpless against them, mostly because we don't know how to fight by their rules. Men are more comfortable with violence. Give us a gun and a license to destroy everything in our path and we'll be just fine. But when it comes to mental warfare, which all relationship fights are, we don't know how to defend ourselves.

It's time to change all that. Don't chance throwing a punch and landing in the slammer. Educate yourself to her strategies and you will be better able to combat them. As in war and sports, the key to victory is to know your enemy and be one step ahead of her. And that's where we can help. Here are just a few of the tactics that women use to start, win, or complicate an argument, as well as defense strategies that you can use to stop them.

TACTIC: Crying. No man can resist a crying woman, and she knows it. A few well-timed tears can turn any argument to her favor, rendering you guilty and confused. Before you know it, you've forgotten why you were arguing with her altogether and will do anything to console her.

DEFENSIVE STRATEGY: Beat her to the punch. If you know she's a crier, don't give her the chance to shed the first tear. Start bawling as soon as an argument begins, catching her off-guard and with little choice but to comfort you and apologize.

TACTIC: The Silent Treatment. You did something wrong and she's not gonna tell you what it is. You'll know there's trouble when she starts giving you icy stares and refuses to answer even the most simple questions. Pretty soon, you'll be jumping through hoops trying to figure out what she's mad about, resulting in an argument where she gets to sit back and relax and you have to do all the work.

DEFENSIVE STRATEGY: If she won't tell you what you did to make her angry, forget it and start from scratch. Do something that you know will infuriate her. Make sexual puns about her sister, draw on the walls, drop your pants and fart, anything that will get a reaction from her. She'll still be mad at you, but at least now you'll know why.

TACTIC: Gibberish. Comments like "I don't think you respect my wallpaper" and "When was the last time you looked in the fridge? No, I mean *really* looked," are just the sort of nonsensical drivel that women like to use to confuse the hell out of us. If we have no idea what they mean, then we can't possibly make amends, so they win automatically. A woman skilled in the art of nonsense can destroy a man every time.

DEFENSIVE STRATEGY: Meet her nonsense with even more nonsense. Demand that she apologize to the dog for having opposable thumbs. Tell her that you don't think she's sensitive to your feelings for the stereo. Start singing "Bess, You Is My Woman" for no apparent reason. Hey, two can play at that game.

TACTIC: Calling Mom. A phone call to Mommy allows her to have an argument with you without even talking to you. You have to sit and listen to her bitch about your faults, without the benefit of being able to dispute them. Also, she has managed to make it two-against-one, odds that you will be unable to beat. If you're really unlucky, she'll put you on the phone and make you talk to the old bat.

DEFENSIVE STRATEGY: You're going to have to prepare for this day well in advance. Make sure that her mom loves you long before your first fight. Take her out to dinner, buy her flowers, do everything in your power to make her think that you're the perfect man. If that doesn't work, you'll have to give your girlfriend a piece of her own medicine. Don't just call your mom, invite her over. When the little lady comes home, your mom will be waiting for her. If she wants to fight via parents, let the witch do it face to face.

TACTIC: Sleeping with Your Friends. If you find her in bed with your best friend, she's probably trying to tell you that she's angry. Anyone who thinks that women don't use sex as a weapon is a deluded fool. They know that we love sex and we're not keen on sharing. If we could, we'd lock up her womanhood in a safe deposit box. Sleeping with strangers is enough to drive us batty, but sleeping with our *friends* is a sure-fire way to render us helpless with jealousy. We'll do anything she wants if she'll only agree to give us sole ownership of her sexual wares.

DEFENSIVE STRATEGY: You can't help but be jealous, but don't let her know that. Pretend that you like it and you'd like her to do more of it. Ask if you can invite some of your closest buds over for her to "service." If she says no, act offended, saying, "If you really loved me, you'd respect my friends." After that, her promiscuity will come to an abrupt end. Cheating ceases to be fun if you actually *enjoy* it.

✳

Making Up (Gifts and Their Side Effects)

The most important aspect of fighting is making up afterward. Short of kissing ass, the best way to show her that you're sorry is to buy her a gift. But not all gifts are created equally and some of them may backfire on you. Let's take a look at some of the most common gifts and how effective they actually are.

GIFT	EFFECTIVENESS	LONG-TERM RESULTS
Flowers	Not very original, but they do the trick. They won't completely undo the damage, but at least she'll think you're not as big a jerk as she originally thought.	She'll put them in a vase and forget about them. In no way will they ensure against future arguments. You're starting from scratch, bubba.
Candy	The way to a woman's heart is through her stomach. Feed her some tasty treats and she'll be too busy digesting to remember why she was mad at you in the first place.	She'll get fat and blame you. If you thought she was mad at you before, you ain't seen nothing yet.
Lingerie	She knows that this is more a gift for you than it is for her. But if she looks good in it, her self-esteem will improve and you'll get some good lovin'.	It will be of no help to you come the next argument. If she's yelling at you, she's not gonna want to slip into a sexy nightie.
Puppy	Puppies are so goddamn cute that they drive women into a state of hysteria. She'll forgive you for everything, and then some, and bow before you as a God among men.	A puppy is just like a baby, except a baby doesn't require long walks and will not chew up all of your good clothes. She'll be so busy keeping an eye on the beast that she won't have time to argue ever again. But then again, she won't have time to have sex ever again either.

Pay for her rent	She'll be too stunned not to forgive you. Granted, it's not too romantic, but you won't see her complaining.	You paid her bills. You *own* her. If she tries getting uppity again, remind her who the sugar daddy is and suggest that she sleep in the streets if she doesn't like it.

Breaking Up

So what happens if you picked the wrong woman and you want out? Breaking up is hard to do, and most of the tried-and-true methods that men have relied on for years don't work anymore. Just saying "it's over" will be met with tears and arguments. Sleeping around on her to make her hate you is bound to backfire. All women are connected to a worldwide network that can tarnish a guy's reputation in no time. No, if you want to break up with a woman, you're gonna have to be tricky about it. The key, of course, is to make *them* break up with *you,* thereby acquitting you of all blame and responsibility.

To get you started, here are a few possibilities that will catch her by surprise and make the painful turn of breaking up easier on you.

Move In

During those fragile first few months of a relationship, a woman is not yet ready to adjust to all of your bad habits. This makes it the perfect time to strike, especially if you're looking for an easy exit. Give her some sob story about being evicted and ask if you can stay at her place for a while until you can find another apartment. Bring over only your most annoying guy accessories: framed

"Quake" posters, tat-
tered underwear, old
Playboys, empty cases of
beer, anything that will
make her uncomfort-
able and possibly even
leave a stench.

Then settle in and
proceed to make a nui-
sance of yourself. Stay drunk all day, order a lot of pay-for-view porn,
and make long distance phone calls to Japan. Pee on the toilet and
leave your clothes scattered all over the floor. If she confronts you,
don't respond by being a jerk. Women know exactly what this
means and they'll refuse to end a relationship on principle alone. Instead, act like a helpless child, scared of the world and unable to take
care of yourself. She'll still resent you, but she'll feel guilty about it,
which is right where you want her.

Start asking for large and unnecessary loans and use the money for
drugs. Burst into tears for no reason and make frequent calls to psy-
chic hotlines. She should find you passed out in your own vomit on
a regular basis. Before long, she won't be able to take it anymore,
and she'll tell you it's over. Drop to your knees and beg for forgive-
ness, making such a spectacle of yourself that she'll wonder why she
ever started dating you in the first place. When she asks you to pack
and get out, don't put up a fight. Just cry and mutter to yourself,
"What am I gonna do?" She'll feel awful for weeks and you'll have
escaped without having to be the bad guy.

Go Insane

Women like men who are on the edge, but there is nothing even re-
motely attractive about an all-out psychopath. She'll turn and run
when you start foaming at the mouth and howling obscenities to un-

seen enemies. But be sure to take your time. No woman is going to believe that you can turn psycho overnight. The transition should take weeks, even months, to complete.

Begin by making occasional odd remarks. For instance, when you're lying in bed with her one night, start screaming, "The walls have eyes! They're staring at me!" When she asks you what's wrong, put her at ease by saying that you've had a stressful week of work. But gradually your bizarre comments should occur more often, and get more and more absurd. When she cooks you dinner, demand that the food be inspected for "demons." When she gets dressed up for a night on the town, accuse her of conspiring against you by wearing the color red, your "sworn arch-nemesis." Lock yourself in the bathroom and refuse to come out until the cat has been shaved. Stop bathing altogether and urinate in every corner of her apartment to mark your territory. Tell her friends that your real name is Zortar, Sun God and Keeper of the Sacred Virgin. Tell her parents that her vagina has been "ordering me to kill." Then one night she'll come home and find you huddled in the corner, naked and covered in ointment, announcing that you have destroyed all of her furniture so that "the gnomes won't get them." You'll be out on the street before you know it.

Scare Her

Sure, a good girlfriend will stick by you when times get tough, but everybody has their limits. Say, for instance, that you show up at her door one night, covered in blood and holding a knife, babbling about "A horrible mistake." Odds are, this relationship is over. Better yet, make it appear that you may soon be the victim of a violent crime. Have your friends dress as mob henchmen and visit her apartment when you're not there. "Just tell him that Vito is looking for him," they'll say, "and he's not happy." When she asks you who these men are, tell her that "there are things about me that you must never know, for your own safety." She may find this sexy at first, in which case you'll have to up the voltage a little. Disappear for days and then show up covered in bruises and scars. Keep her curtains shut, the lights low, and wear only black. Carry a shotgun with you at all times and fire wildly at the slightest noise. Scream at her when she tries to go near the closet, saying that you have yet to "dispose of" its contents. Talk in your sleep, alternating between delirious sobs and muttering, "The horror, the horror . . ." Any woman with a reasonable sense of self-preservation will tell you to leave and never come back.

Die

Dying is, by far, the best way to end a relationship. But it isn't the most popular option, as death makes future dating almost impossible. It is quite enough that she simply *hears* that you have died. Under no circumstances does she need to find your cold corpse lying in a bathtub filled with blood to believe that you are really dead. All you need is a witness, a phony death certificate, and a mock funeral. This can be accomplished with the help of your friends and the willing cooperation of a dirty funeral director or mortician (grease their palms and anything is possible).

She will probably be curious about how you died, so give special attention to concocting a good story. Something romantic like "He fought for your honor against a group of ruthless thugs" sounds better than "He stiffed a pimp on a coke deal." If she really cared about you, give her something nice to remember you by. We're talking mementos here, not money. A shoe should be enough. Or one of your old sweaters. Something that smells like you. Chicks like that.

※ But what if,
God forbid,
she breaks up with
YOU? ※

Yes, believe it or not, it does happen. Even to guys like you. In fact, *especially* to guys like you. It's one of the harsh realities of dating that few of us think will happen to us, but always does. You could be the sweetest, most loving boyfriend in the world, generous to a fault and adored by women everywhere. But that doesn't protect you from the merciless sucker punch that is being dumped. Nothing stings more than getting your walking papers from a woman just when you thought everything in your relationship was going peachy. It can be a humiliating experience to be rejected by your lover, mostly because you didn't get the chance to reject *her* first.

Even though we're always surprised when the hammer comes down, we really shouldn't be. Most times, women send early warning signs that a relationship is headed for derailment. We may not be alert enough to pick up on them, and sometimes we just choose to ignore them. But we cannot deny that the majority of women will let us know that all is not well in paradise. Here are just a few of the indicators women use to let us know that the end is nigh.

- She's been talking more and more about grad school.
- She has slowly but surely been moving her things back to her place.
- She makes vague remarks that "We need to talk."
- She acts offended when you try to touch her.
- She's stopped having sex with you.

- She gets irritated with you for "breathing too loud."
- You haven't seen her in over a week.
- She's started calling you "Tubby."
- Lots 'n' lots of cold, icy stares.

So what can you do to protect yourself? Actually, nothing. Once a woman has decided to let you go, there isn't much you can do to change her mind. Do both of you a favor and *deal with it.* Suck it up, Alvy Singer, you're a big boy now. You can't always get what you want, and that's just too fucking bad. You can make a scene, bitch and moan, and beg her to reconsider. But this will only make the whole breakup that much more mortifying for you, and will only remind her of why she wanted to dump you in the first place.

Speaking of her reasons, forget about trying to understand them. A woman does not always have a rational explanation for why she doesn't want to date a guy anymore. Love is not particularly rational anyway, so why should the breakup be any better? To give you a taste of just how random and nonsensical they can be, we talked to some recently emancipated women and asked them to explain why they dumped their respective beaus. Here is what they told us . . .

"He had weird-looking ankles."
"He couldn't sit still."
"He'd always sing off-key."
"He didn't own a suit."
"His cat shed too much."
"He drank too much coffee."
"He lost the remote control to my TV and didn't buy me a new one."
"My best friend didn't like him."
"My best friend never met him."
"My best friend just had a bad feeling about him."

"He didn't speak Portuguese."

"He laughed at things that I didn't find funny."

"He wore briefs instead of boxers."

"When the light shone on him in a certain way, he looked just like a Muppet."

"He had bad posture."

"His butt was too tiny."

"His butt was too lumpy."

"His butt wasn't attached to Brad Pitt."

"My horoscope told me to break up with him."

"He liked the new 'Star Trek' better than the old 'Star Trek.' "

"His teeth made me uncomfortable."

"He didn't wear enough ties."

"His eyes were too shifty."

"His apartment smelled like my grandmother's house."

"His aura was all wrong."

Once you've resigned yourself to the unpredictable nature of breakups, you may find yourself consumed with feelings of helplessness and despair. This is a perfectly natural reaction. Nobody likes to think that they're powerless, especially in relationships. But just because you can't control her actions doesn't mean that you should feel completely impotent. There are ways to make yourself feel better and begin the healing process. Here are just a few:

1. Drink heavily. Your first instinct will be to get piss-drunk and stay that way, and you should definitely not resist that temptation. After what that hussy did to you, you deserve to drown your sorrows in a bottle and make an ass out of yourself. But alcohol does more than numb your senses to the mind-boggling pain of heartbreak. It also allows you to openly embrace your self-obsessed mood swings. You can weep and howl, talk endlessly about the breakup with your friends, and plot every sort of revenge that you'll inevitably forget about when you sober up. Nobody will be able to blame you for your pathetic behavior. After all, you're obviously too intoxicated to realize what a tiresome bore you've become. Best of all, alcohol gives you the irresistible urge to break things. There's no better way to get rid of your pent-up hostility than by causing severe structural damage. Break some bottles, bust a chair or two, knock over a table. Anything that isn't nailed down can, and should, be thrown across the room. But if you're gonna bust some shit up, make sure you're not at home when you do it. Nothing kills a buzz faster than realizing that you've just trashed your entire apartment. Also, remember to take your anger out on objects, not people. With your stupid luck, you'll end up smacking around the biggest guy in the bar. And then you'll have a broken jaw to go along with your heart.

2. Lie to your friends. Your ego has been bruised enough as it is, you don't need to make matters worse by telling your friends the truth about your breakup. Don't try to pass off one of those "It was a mutual decision" explanations. Everybody knows that it's bullshit. If you really want to save face, insist that it was you, not her, who ended the relationship. Sure, it's a big fat lie, but what does that matter? It's your word against hers, and it's not like being honest is going to make her come back to you. After the deed has been done, it's all just semantics anyway. So go ahead, spread around your inaccurate version of the separation. You'll feel like less of a schmuck and after a while you might even start to believe it yourself. But it doesn't have to stop there. As long as you're trashing her name, you might as well go whole hog with it. Spread some rumors that will *really* damage her reputation. Tell your friends that she has a drinking problem, casually mention that she wears a hairpiece or has a superfluous nipple, and let everybody know that "I'll miss her, but I sure won't miss her genital warts." Odds are, nobody will believe you anyway. But if just one of your evil lies gets repeated and, glory upon glories, even gets back to her, there is no sweeter revenge in the world.

3. Sleep with a stranger. There's nothing better for what ails you than a bout of animalistic, emotionless sex with a woman you've never met before and have no intention of ever seeing again. It's a "Wham bam" without the "Thank you, ma'am." Although primarily used to distract you from the pain of heartbreak, sex with a stranger also serves to remind you that your ex-girlfriend was not the end of your love life. The biggest fear that most men experience after being dumped is "Will I ever get laid again?" You need to remind yourself that you are still capable of attracting the opposite sex and, more important, that there are other woman out there willing to touch your penis. Pretty much any partner will do, but try to practice a little discretion in your selection. You don't want to end up in bed with a close friend or friend's girlfriend. There's a big difference between enjoying a night of unfettered sleaze and being a complete moron. And make sure that your one-night lover understands your intentions and wants to take part. There are plenty of fish in the sea, and many of them are hanging around bars just waiting for a meaningless quickie with someone they don't have to call the next day. If all else fails, find a prostitute and spend some cash on your nookie. Sure, it's a pathetic solution, but you're feeling pathetic anyway, so why not?

4. Leave town. That's right, get the hell outta Dodge. Hit the road and don't tell anybody where you're going. All of your friends will be worried sick about you, and substantially more sympathetic about the breakup than if you stuck around and whined to them about it. When your ex-girlfriend finds out that you've disappeared, she may even feel a touch of remorse that she wouldn't have experienced otherwise. Leaving town has all of the advantages of suicide but without any of the permanence or mess. But more impor-

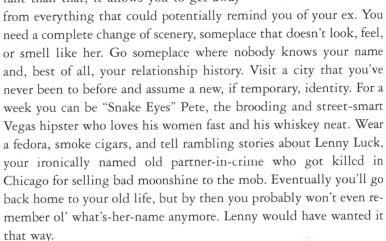

tant than that, it allows you to get away from everything that could potentially remind you of your ex. You need a complete change of scenery, someplace that doesn't look, feel, or smell like her. Go someplace where nobody knows your name and, best of all, your relationship history. Visit a city that you've never been to before and assume a new, if temporary, identity. For a week you can be "Snake Eyes" Pete, the brooding and street-smart Vegas hipster who loves his women fast and his whiskey neat. Wear a fedora, smoke cigars, and tell rambling stories about Lenny Luck, your ironically named old partner-in-crime who got killed in Chicago for selling bad moonshine to the mob. Eventually you'll go back home to your old life, but by then you probably won't even remember ol' what's-her-name anymore. Lenny would have wanted it that way.

5. Write a book about dating and besmirch her name. It's actually much easier than you'd think. First you convince a publisher to let you write a funny book about dating. Then find a reason to mock her somewhere in the book, possibly using her as an example of "evil girlfriends." If you don't want to be that subtle, you can just come right out and trash her for no reason whatsoever. For example:

EX-GIRLFRIEND OF AUTHOR*	PERSONAL FLAWS
Stephanie	Arrogant, hypocritical, vain, cheats on her boyfriends, a feminist for all the wrong reasons, bad hair
Sally	Unambitious, despondent, inanimate, pot head, big forehead, sleeps a lot
Karen	Self-righteous, possessive, judgmental, demanding, hyena-like laugh, actually thought Marilyn Monroe was an "artist"
Claudia	naive, moody, cowardly, two-dimensional, tendency to whine, has an annoying family, too young

Yeah, yeah, we know. That's an awfully immature and mean-spirited thing to do. We've probably caused these poor women an undue amount of public embarrassment. Do they deserve to be openly slandered just because they happened to dump a grudge-holding author? You may be right, we are being unfair. But guess what? We don't really care.

* In most cases, the names have been changed to protect the innocent. Except for Stephanie. She really deserves to be humiliated in print. By the way, she lives in Wisconsin, she used to be a beauty queen, and her last name rhymes with "pet."

Commitment
and Other Things That
Scare the Shit Outta Us

It's often been said that women fall in love faster, but men fall harder. It's true, we do take our sweet time giving in to our emotions. But when we finally do fall in love, it hits us like a speeding truck and spills our guts all over the highway for everybody to see. It can be an unsettling experience, especially for women. They aren't accustomed to guys in love and they aren't sure how to react to them. A love-struck fella is likely to be affectionate, dedicated, passionate, sensitive, understanding, romantic, and everything else that women want from men but never expect to actually get from them. For many women, it can be like encountering a dog that can sing opera. They're delighted that it's learned how to do something more interesting than lick its balls. But still . . . *what the fuck?*

Guys and love get along just fine. Contrary to popular belief, we aren't afraid of it. As a matter of fact, we're big fans of the world's most sought-after emotion. And why wouldn't we be? As far as good feelings are concerned, love is pretty much the top of the mountain.

It's the ultimate high, better than anything you could get from drugs or even sex. Yes, you heard right. Love is better than sex. In fact, love is so far out of sex's league that it seems silly to even compare them. Anybody who says that this isn't true has probably never actually been in love, or has had some really, *really* amazing sex.

So let's forget about love for the moment. Love is easy. We all want it and, if we're lucky, we'll get it someday. Guys don't have a problem with love. What we have a problem with is the flip-side of love. It's that irritating buzz-kill known as

Commitment.

There's just something about commitment that scares us silly. There's something so ominous about it, so irreversible, so terrifyingly permanent. Many of us would rather take a bullet in the gut than willingly submit ourselves to a relationship commitment. We don't really like committing to anything, much less a woman. If it was up to us, everything in life would be noncommittal. All homes would be rented, not owned. All careers would be temporary, not full time. And everything you owned would come with a money-back guarantee, no questions asked. To us, it just seems easier that way.

Having said that, we must also point out that guys have gotten a bad rap when it comes to commitment. We'll admit that we're not eager to commit to a woman, but that doesn't mean we don't intend to eventually. We know that a commitment is necessary if we ever want to have a substantial relationship with a woman. But we want to play the market a little bit first, check out the selection, sow our oats, pump out the jams, get the funk out—you know how it is. Sooner or later, every single one of us intends to pick a Ms. Right and call off the party. We don't like the idea of growing old alone any more than the gentle gender. We just want to be *sure* before we sign on the dotted line.

To be fair, it isn't only men who have a problem with commitment. An awful lot of women out there aren't quite as eager to make a final choice as they would have us believe. We've all heard the excuses they give. "This is moving too fast." "I need some 'me' time." "I want to establish my career first." "I need some space." "You're suffocating me." "I've changed the locks." "Stop calling me, you freak." "I've got a restraining order." "Back off or I'll cut you."

Regardless of what women say, they're as uncomfortable with commitment as we are. They're in touch with their needs and pity the fool who tries to break down the walls of their fortress of self-absorption. Oh sure, there are a few good apples out there who actually *know* what they want and are ready to stick by it when they find it. But those women are, as the old cliché goes, either married or gay.

But we can point all the fingers we want, it won't do us a bit of good. Even though commitment anxiety is a malady shared by both sexes, we're only responsible for our own actions. If guys want to put a stake in the heart of commitment fear, we need to start with ourselves. Let the women take care of their own neuroses, we've got plenty of our own to worry about. So sit your butt down, get a stiff drink, and let's figure out what we can do to put an end to this bullshit once and for all.

There is only one good reason not to commit to a woman: You no longer want to be in a relationship with her. That's it, guys. There's no middle ground. After a relationship reaches a certain point, you either move ahead or call it quits. But too often we want to have our cake and eat it too, so we'll come up with all sorts of excuses not to commit. We don't want to lose our girlfriends, but we don't want any guarantees that they're going to stick around either. To put it bluntly, we're pussies.

Well that's about to end, right here, right now. It's time to nip that shit in the bud. We're not going to coddle you. We're not going to be patient with you. You've gotten plenty of that sympathetic crap from everybody else, but we're not going to let you off so easy. We're going to dish out the tough love. If you're ever going to change your ramblin' ways, you need firm advice without the hand-holding. You need a bitch slap of reality. And we're just the guys to give it to you.

TYPICAL COMMITMENT FEAR	A BITCH SLAP OF REALITY
"There might be somebody better out there."	Even if there is, what makes you think that she'll want to go out with you? Get it through your thick skull, tough guy. Not every woman in the world wants you. In fact, very few of them do. If you're lucky enough to find a woman willing to stay with you, consider yourself fortunate.
"I'm not ready to give up my independence."	For most guys, independence means living alone in a roach-infested studio apartment, a steady diet of alcohol and microwave foods, and contracting sexual diseases from indifferent partners. If that's the life you want, you're welcome to it.
"It'll get boring having sex with the same person all the time."	You're lucky to be having any sex at all, so quit bitching and count your blessings, kahuna.
"What if I let myself be vulnerable and she dumps me?"	A wise man once said, "It is better to have loved and lost than never to have loved at all." Or as we once said, "Shut your stinking pie-hole and deal with it." Yeah, you might get hurt. But so fucking what? Take a chance for once and see what happens. Unless you're more comfortable with the idea of going to your grave with the knowledge that you were a coward.

"She expects too much from me. I don't want the responsibility of being her boyfriend."	You're a big boy now, bubba. It's time to accept a little responsibility and act like a goddamn adult. Sure, it's hard work to be in a relationship. But only sissy-boys complain about it. Everything worthwhile in life is difficult to keep. If it wasn't, every lard-butt like you could have whatever he wanted. But that ain't gonna happen. Sorry to burst your bubble.
"What if I start to feel suffocated by the relationship?"	And just what the hell is *that* supposed to mean? Could you be a little more vague maybe? If you're feeling suffocated, open a window and loosen your collar. Anything else is just a piss-poor excuse for running away from a relationship. If you're gonna be a schmuck, at least get a better excuse than that.
"I'm afraid that dating her will cause me to lose my identity."	So let's get this straight: You're afraid that she's gonna pull an Eleanor Roosevelt on you and overshadow your own accomplishments? Did it ever occur to you that maybe she *is* more interesting than you? Maybe your identity pales in comparison to hers. If you know what's good for you, you'll stay with her, unless you're keen on a lifetime of obscurity.
"I don't want to stick around long enough to watch her grow old and ugly."	And you're going to be a pretty-looking old man, is that it? If she's willing to watch you become a balding, pot-bellied, impotent old geezer, then you can put up with her sagging tits.

Once you've managed to quit stalling and commit to a relation-ship, you'll find that it really isn't such a bad place to be in after all. It's easy to become accustomed to the life of a steady boyfriend. You

always have a date for the weekends, there's someone to share the good times and the bad times, and you're getting laid on a fairly regular ba-sis. It's a cozy, secure feeling that has caused many men to wonder why they wasted so much of their life being single.

But just when you think you've got everything in your love life under control, you could be headed straight for trouble with a cap-ital T. As far as you're concerned, everything is better than ever. You and your little woman are happy as clams, living out a dream of re-lationship bliss and harmony. But what you don't know is that sometimes relationships are not always what they seem. Sometimes a commitment can be taken too far, often with perilous results. You think you're in love, but the rest of the world knows

You've Been Pussy-whipped!

Most of you are probably a lit-tle confused and alarmed by this. "Wait a minute," you say. "You just bullied us into a commitment and now you're saying we're whipped because of it? What are you doing to us? Are you trying to screw with our heads? Fuck you, we're outta here!" Well hold on. Before you run off in a huff, let us explain.

Relationships are not as easy as saying, "Hey, can I play too?" and then joining the fun. If you've managed to make it this far, we congratulate you. But there are still a few dangers that you need to become aware of, and we're only trying to help you steer clear of them. So calm your silly ass down and listen to what we have to say. A cliché or not, many guys do become pussy-whipped and it has ruined their relationships. Whatever your opinions may be on this very real phenomenon, you owe it to yourself to take a moment and examine this strange and terrifying disease in more detail.

What Exactly Do We Mean by "Pussy-whipped?"

Technically, it has nothing to do with pussy. A guy who is pussy-whipped is getting as much or little pussy as any other guy with a girlfriend. It actually has more to do with the relationship itself than anything genital-related. Pussy-whipped is a condition wherein a man has become obsessive about a relationship. He has been "whipped" into submitting completely to the every whim of his lover. In most cases, relationships are a wonderful, enriching experience. But like anything in life, if you start to take it too seriously and let yourself be dominated by it, you will become a pitiful junkie.

A healthy relationship depends on the realization that your girlfriend is just *one part* of your life. But the pussy-whipped man is unable to make this distinction, and like the worst addict, he just wants more, more, *more!* Before long he won't even leave his apartment anymore, content to stay inside and enjoy the pleasant, numbing buzz that only his relationship can provide. He's intoxicated by the security and familiarity of it, soothed by the predictable routine of life with his significant other. He has become, quite literally, attached to his girlfriend at the hip. And as anyone who has witnessed this kind of mutated freak can tell you, it's very difficult for them to move without falling on their ass.

In some cases, the relationship of a pussy-whipped man can become abusive. He doesn't make a move without her consent, his every thought and action has been predetermined and approved by her, and he wouldn't dream of going anywhere without her. He is trapped inside an Orwellian nightmare and doesn't even know it. More often than not, the girlfriend is not to blame for this situation. She is just as manipulated by the relationship as he is. Although they are both responsible for giving life to this beast, neither of them has any real control over it. Occasionally you will find a woman who is aware of her power and enjoys wielding it, but this occurs only in rare cases and the guy usually wises up after a while. But the most common and also most dangerous cases are those where both partners have the best of intentions and just don't realize what they are doing to each other.

If you're like most guys, you probably don't think that you're whipped. This is because most of us have been falsely accused at one time or another, usually by a jealous buddy. A typical exchange looks something like this:

BUDDY: You wanna go out and get some beers?
YOU: Not tonight. I have a date.
BUDDY: You're whipped, man.

This so-called buddy is obviously just upset that you have blown him off for another woman. But if the tables were turned and *he* was the one with the date, he'd probably do the same thing to you. The sad fact is, single guys don't like it when their friends are getting laid. As a result, the majority of whipped accusations are just thinly veiled attacks on the good luck of men who've managed to get a girlfriend.

But this is not always the case. Sometimes whipped accusations are right on the money and we just don't want to admit it. For instance:

BUDDY: You wanna go out and get some beers?

YOU: Uh, yeah, but . . . I gotta ask my girlfriend if it's okay.

BUDDY: You're whipped, man.

And he's right. You *are* whipped.

Hopefully we have made you pause and think. "Am I a victim of pussy-whipping? And if so, what can I do to make it stop?" Well hold on there, Tex. Slow down a little. The first step to recovery is admitting that you have a problem, and we don't know if you do yet. It's difficult to determine whether or not you are actually whipped. You can't trust your own judgment, and you certainly don't want to listen to the opinions of your guy friends. To aid you in this process, we've put together a short quiz that will determine once and for all if you are indeed whipped. So take out a number-two pencil, ask your lady friend to leave the room for a minute, and answer these questions *honestly.*

We're only trying to help, fellas.

Quiz: Are you whipped?

1. How often do you tell her that you love her?
   a. Every once in a while
   b. At least once a day
   c. Every other minute

2. How often are you together?
   a. You see her a couple times a week
   b. You see her all the time, and spend major holidays with her
   c. You don't go to the bathroom without her

3. **What best describes a typical date?**
   a. A movie and a few beers at the local bar
   b. A fancy restaurant
   c. A pizza and "Must-See" TV

4. **When people meet you on the street, they usually ask you . . .**
   a. "Are you still dating that girl?"
   b. "How's the ol' ball 'n' chain treating you?"
   c. "I thought you were married."

5. **Who are your friends?**
   a. All of your friends are also her friends
   b. All of your friends are other couples
   c. You haven't seen anybody but her for months

6. **How much do you share with each other?**
   a. Most of your stuff is at her place, or vice versa
   b. You bought a major purchase together, like a VCR or a car
   c. You have a joint checking account

7. **A favorite topic of discussion for you and your girlfriend is . . .**
   a. World politics
   b. What to do for your anniversary
   c. Who looks cuter

8. **Have you planned for the future?**
   a. You've discussed moving in together
   b. You've discussed marriage
   c. You've already decided on the names of your first three kids

9. How has your social life changed?
   a. You still go out drinking with the boys
   b. You have a special night for going out drinking with the boys
   c. You now go out drinking with the girls

10. What best describes your sex life?
   a. Hot, nasty, and better than ever
   b. Overly familiar, but still exciting
   c. A pizza and "Must-See" TV

SCORING: Give yourself 5 points every time you picked "a," 10 points for "b," and 15 points for "c."

0–50   You've got nothing to worry about. You are in no danger of being whipped.
55–100   Close call, but you're not whipped. Not yet anyway. Watch your step.
105–150   Sound the alarms. You're whipped, man.

If it turns out that you qualify as pussy-whipped, your first reaction may be one of denial. There's nothing wrong with that. Go ahead and get it out of your system. Throw the book across the room and accuse the authors of conspiring against you. Do the test over and over again until you get it right. Cuddle with your sweetheart and say, "Isn't that funny? They're *satirizing* us." We all have our ways of dealing with a distressing discovery.

But after a while it should sink in and you'll realize that we were right all along. And then you may find yourself being stricken by panic. "How could this happen to me?" you'll say. "I'm a freak, a deformed leper of love. I don't deserve to be in a relationship. I'm going to become a recluse and never show my face to civilized humanity again." Or something like that. It may be more along the lines of, "I'm whipped, huh? Well, that sucks." But the sentiment is the same.

The first thing you want to do is relax. There's no reason to be alarmed. You're not the first guy to discover that he's pussy-whipped, and you certainly won't be the last. It is nothing to be ashamed of, as long as you take the necessary steps to alleviate it. One of the good things about being pussy-whipped is that it's not a fatal disease. It is highly treatable, as long as you want to be cured.

Here are just a few of the methods you can employ to relieve yourself of the painful whipping illness:

1. Get a life. The most common reason that guys become whipped is because they have no life outside of their relationship. Believe it or not, the world is actually bigger than your girlfriend's apartment. Take some time away from her and explore it. Meet new people, try new things, have a few experiences that don't involve your significant other. You can still go back to her at the end of the day, but this time you'll have more to talk about than how much you love each other. If your girlfriend resists your attempts to have a life without her, remind her that a healthy relationship depends on trust. As a man named Sting once said, "If you love somebody, set them free." Of course, Sting is also responsible for the memorable quote "De Do Do Do, De Da Da Da is all I want to say to you," so he may not have any idea what he's talking about. The point is, don't let her misgivings dissuade you. All girlfriend and no life make Jack a dull boy.

2. Get some balls. Guys are only human, so like most people, we like to think that we're not responsible for our own faults. If we're pussy-whipped, it must be the woman's fault, right? Unfortunately, that's hardly ever the case. A guy can't be pussy-whipped without his consent, which makes us accomplices in the crime. If you really want to stop being whipped, the best place to start is with yourself. Take a closer look at what you're doing, how you're acting, what kind of signals you're giving her. Most of the time, all you need do to bring an end to whipdom is to stop *encouraging* it. Be the one to initiate spending some time apart. Don't jump to attention every time she speaks. Try using the word "No" occasionally. And for god's sake, stop treating your relationship like it's the center of the universe. She may be alarmed at first by your newfound assertiveness, but eventually she'll get used to it. And if she has any sense of right and wrong, she'll realize that it's for the best.

3. Get rid of her. Every once in a while, a guy will find himself in a relationship with a bona fide she-devil. There are women out there who are actually *responsible* for pussy-whipping and will fight like rabid dogs to keep their guys under their thumb. If you attempt to use either of the two pussy-whipped remedies listed above and she responds by telling you to "shut your trap and give me a massage," then you're probably dealing with a woman who likes having control over you. You could stick around and see if things get better, but sooner or later you're gonna have to face facts. You picked a loser and you're better off without her. Don't be a fool and think you can change her. A woman who has become intoxicated by the thrill of ordering a guy around is not likely to quit just because he's wised up. An abusive girlfriend is to the pussy-whipped man what Hitler was to Germany. You may think that she's acting in your best interest, but she's actually leading you straight for destruction. Do yourself a favor and remove her from power as quickly as possible.

Living in Sin

The time will come when you and your sweetie will want to take your relationship to the next level and shack up together. But before you do so, you should take the time to consider the pros and cons of living together. We had intended to do a lot of research for this section, finding all sorts of facts and figures about cohabitation. But quite frankly, we just didn't have it in us. It's been a really long week and we've just been too lazy to do any real work. We managed to skim through a few newspapers and magazines, but we didn't find anything that was particularly interesting. We had almost given up this chapter for dead when we realized that we knew a person who would be more than willing to do all of our homework for us. She is the ideal research assistant. An investigative reporter of the most inexpensive kind. We know her as . . .

Spitznagel's Mom

Co-author Eric Spitznagel has a mother well known for her fondness for information retrieval. For most of his life, young Spitznagel needed only to make a passing remark on a subject, something like, "Gosh, I don't think pot is so bad for your health." And in a week or two, his mom would deliver to him a mountain of newspaper clippings on marijuana and its effects on the body. Nobody in the Spitznagel family seems to know why she does this. The clippings are almost never requested, but she always takes painstaking efforts to collect them anyway.

"She's like a Lexis/Nexis gone berserk," said one family member who wishes to remain nameless. "If she thinks that you're uninformed about something, she can manage to dig up a staggering amount of data. There's no stopping her."

We decided to find out if Spitznagel's mom could help us with our current drought of information. Spitznagel called his mom at home and casually mentioned that he was writing a chapter on co-habitation but couldn't find anything relevant to say about it. After a couple of weeks, he called back to see if the seed he planted had grown. Not at all to his surprise, it had.

MOM: Hello?
SPITZNAGEL: Hi, Mom. It's me.
MOM: Oh, hello, dear. How's the book coming along?
SPITZNAGEL: It's okay. We're still trying to find some-

thing interesting to say about cohabitation. Have you found any clippings that might be useful to us?

MOM: As a matter of fact, I have. Hold on a minute. *(She gathers together her clippings.)* Okay, I thought this was kind of surprising. Did you know that more young people are living together these days than ever before?

SPITZNAGEL: Is that right?

MOM: Yes. It says here that about 3.3 million households are shared by a man and woman who are not married. There were only about 500,000 couples doing it in 1970.

SPITZNAGEL: So would you say that it's become "hep"?

MOM: Hep?

SPITZNAGEL: Yeah, you know. Is it chillin', phat, and funky fresh?

MOM: What on earth does that mean?

SPITZNAGEL: Never mind. So you're basically telling us that living together is very popular among young people.

MOM: Well, that's what it says here.

SPITZNAGEL: Have you found any articles that would suggest that living together is a bad idea?

MOM: Oh yes, I've found plenty of that.

SPITZNAGEL: How did I know.

MOM: Did you realize that in some parts of the country it's legal for landlords to turn down potential tenants if they're an unmarried couple.

SPITZNAGEL: That's certainly alarming. Where is that happening?

MOM: Well, the article I found says that it recently happened in Wheaton, Illinois.

SPITZNAGEL: Wheaton, huh? Anyplace else?

MOM: It only mentions Wheaton.

SPITZNAGEL: So as far as you know, unmarried couples are only being banned in Wheaton, right?

MOM: Yes, as far as I know. But I'm sure that's not the only place.

SPITZNAGEL: Please, Mom. We only want the facts.

MOM: I guess it's only in Wheaton.

SPITZNAGEL: That's no big deal then. Who wants to live in Wheaton? What's there to do in Wheaton anyway?

MOM: I don't know, dear.

SPITZNAGEL: So if couples steer clear of Wheaton, they should be okay.

MOM: I don't think that's what it means.

SPITZNAGEL: Let's move on. What else have you found for us?

MOM: I found an article that says if couples live together for more than a year, they automatically become common-law marriages.

SPITZNAGEL: Where's that happening? In Wheaton?

MOM: No. Cut that out. I mean all over.

SPITZNAGEL: Any specifics?

MOM: No, I don't think so. *(Sound of ruffling paper.)* It just says all over.

SPITZNAGEL: I know that's not true in San Francisco.

MOM: I suppose not.

SPITZNAGEL: Then "all over" is not necessarily true, is it?

MOM: Okay.

SPITZNAGEL: But you would recommend that couples check the cohabitation laws in their state before shacking up?

MOM: I would think that's a good idea. This article gives the impression that it's happening a lot.

SPITZNAGEL: Anything else our readers should look out for?

MOM: There was a scary article I found about living together and divorce.

SPITZNAGEL: Could you elaborate?

MOM: It says that people who live together before getting married are more likely to get a divorce than couples who don't live together.

SPITZNAGEL: Aw come on, I don't believe that.

MOM: It says so right here. If it wasn't true, they wouldn't put it in the paper.

SPITZNAGEL: What newspaper did you get this from?

MOM: *The Detroit Free Press.*

SPITZNAGEL: I rest my case.

MOM: It's a very good paper.

SPITZNAGEL: According to who?

MOM: Listen, I'll read it to you. "People who live together before tying the knot are more apt to fail in marriage than couples who move in after exchanging vows."

SPITZNAGEL: I still don't believe it. Did they offer any proof?

MOM: Yes. It says that they got this information from a recent study.

SPITZNAGEL: What kind of study?

MOM: Now how would I know that? It's just a study. It says so right here. "In a recent study."

SPITZNAGEL: Who conducted the study? Do you have a name?

MOM: Wait a minute. *(Pause. She looks for a name.)* He's a sociologist by the name of William Axinn.

SPITZNAGEL: Axinn? Isn't that a laundry detergent?

MOM: No, you're thinking of Ajax.

SPITZNAGEL: Whatever. I still think he's full of it.

MOM: Well, I have another article that says young people

are living together instead of getting married because they're afraid of divorce.

SPITZNAGEL: Oh yeah? Why's that?

MOM: Because all of their parents got divorces and they didn't like it.

SPITZNAGEL: That's a pretty good reason.

MOM: You're not afraid of divorce, are you?

SPITZNAGEL: No, Mom. Not at all.

MOM: I was just wondering. Are you going to come visit sometime?

SPITZNAGEL: Yes. But let's stick to the matter at hand. What else have you found for us?

MOM: That's about it. Although I did see a wonderful interview on TV with Danny DeVito and Rhea Pearlman.

SPITZNAGEL: What does that have to do with cohabitation?

MOM: Well, Mr. DeVito said that he and Rhea lived together for eleven years before getting married.

SPITZNAGEL: Is that right? And have they gotten divorced?

MOM: No.

SPITZNAGEL: Doesn't that prove that living together doesn't necessarily lead to divorce?

MOM: I guess you're right. I think he's a wonderful actor.

SPITZNAGEL: He's a midget.

MOM: He is not a midget. He's just short.

SPITZNAGEL: Whatever.

MOM: Come to think of it, his wife Rhea is pretty short too.

SPITZNAGEL: Do you think that has anything to do with their success at living together?

MOM: I don't know. It couldn't hurt.

SPITZNAGEL: How's that?

MOM: Well, all of their furniture could be the same size.

SPITZNAGEL: You're right.

MOM: I'm sure that it makes things more comfortable.

SPITZNAGEL: That's a good point.

MOM: I wish I had more to tell you.

SPITZNAGEL: That's okay, Mom. You did great.

MOM: Okay. I'll keep looking if you want.

SPITZNAGEL: No, no. You got everything we need.

MOM: Do you think the book is going to do well?

SPITZNAGEL: I don't know, Mom. We'll see.

MOM: I hope so. If the book does well, your father really wants some tickets to the Chicago Bulls.

SPITZNAGEL: I know, he's told me.

MOM: I just think it'd be sweet if you could buy him some Bulls tickets.

SPITZNAGEL: We'll see.

A Short Summary of What Spitznagel's Mom Has Taught Us About Cohabitation

1. Living together outside of marriage is more popular than ever among young people.

2. It is a bad idea to live in Wheaton, Illinois.

3. Some state laws will consider couples "common-law marriages" if they live together for too long.

4. A lot of young people are afraid of divorce.

5. In Detroit, they think that living with a woman will lead to divorce.

6. Danny DeVito and Rhea Pearlman have single-handedly disproved this theory.

7. Couples have a better chance of successfully living together if they're the same height.

8. Spitznagel's dad needs Bulls tickets.

Now that you know all the facts, you should be ready to make an intelligent decision about whether or not you want to live with your girlfriend. And as long as you don't live in Wheaton, Illinois, it's probably a good idea. The advantages of living together are obvious. Your rent will be cheaper, all of your stuff will be in one place, and you'll finally have a roommate whom you can share *everything* with. No more arguments about who ate whose food, or whose turn it is to clean the bathroom. Well, you may have a few of those. But at least women are a little cleaner and won't piss all over the bathroom floor.

That being said, we should also point out that there is a difficult side to living with a woman. They may not be as hygienically challenged as your old guy roommates, but they can often be as troublesome to co-exist with peacefully. If you want to make your new home a happy one, you should give some serious thought to what you can do to make your girlfriend feel more comfortable. When you get down to basics, it really isn't that hard to get along with a live-in lover. There are a few simple rules that will guarantee domestic bliss for as long as you share an apartment together. Study these rules well. Many of them directly contradict some fundamental male instincts and they may take some time for you to get used to. But if you can handle them, you will soon be enjoying the fruits of cohabitation.

The Rules for Living with a Woman

1. Clean up after yourself. Guys don't understand the meaning of dirt. We don't know what's wrong with a little rotting food in the fridge or soap scum on the bathroom wall. Well, it's about time we learned better. Dirt is bad. Dirt is something that should be cleaned up or disposed of. It's ugly and disease-ridden and tends to attract unwanted guests like cockroaches. Although guys often don't have a problem with cockroaches (we consider them visiting friends who don't drink our beer), women find them repulsive. And you don't get rid of cockroaches by squashing them with your foot. You get rid of them by throwing out your trash or cleaning up dirt. Even though the refrigerator is relatively safe from cockroaches, it is another area of the apartment that should be cleaned every so often. Throw out anything that's expired or stinks, and don't store exposed food in there. It's called "botulism," fellas, look it up.

2. Don't hog the TV. This may seem like a inane rule, but trust us, it's important. The television is often the source of most cohabitation distress. When you were living with just guys, you could probably all agree on what programs to watch. But women and men enjoy very different types of TV shows, and it's essential that you find a way to compromise. A day will come when she wants to  watch her soaps but you were hoping to take in that Adam Sandler film festival on HBO. If you haven't agreed on a fair way to divvy

up TV time beforehand, you could find yourself involved in a bru-
tal argument that both of you know is stupid but yet neither of you
is willing to back down from. Find a way to share the TV so that
you're both happy, and do it before a conflict arises. If you want to
watch the NBA Playoffs tonight, let her watch that romantic tear-
jerker with Demi Moore and the dead guy tomorrow.

3. Don't be a jerk. It's as simple as that, and yet for so many
guys, it's just too difficult. Pay your half of the bills, try to stay
sober, and don't smack her around. Yes, we know that it can be
tough to live with someone. But this is not your typical roommate
situation. You're no longer living with "Slappy" Joe, your old buddy
from college. This is supposedly the woman you love. Treat her with
a little respect and patience, and you'll get the same in return. You'd
be surprised at how well women respond to guys who are *nice* to
them, and this is especially true in your situation. She can be as irritated by living with you as you are with her, but sometimes a few
kind and gentle words are all it takes to smooth things over and
make everything right again. If she's getting on your nerves so much
that you can't even talk to her anymore, just leave for a while. Take
a walk, do some shopping, or go hang out with the boys. Or better
yet, go into a different room and slam the door. It's a good idea to
get an apartment that has a few extra rooms in it, or else you'll have
to retreat to the bathroom every time you get fed up with her. And
let's face it, there are only so many hours in the day that you can
spend on the can.

4. Always put the toilet seat down. For some reason, this is
something that women feel particularly adamant about. We've never
seen a woman more furious and offended as when a man doesn't put
the toilet seat back down after taking a whiz. Personally, we don't
know what the big deal is. Could there be anything *more* antifeminist than this? What's the problem, ladies? Are your hands too

dainty to handle the complex machinery of a toilet seat? If women are so keen on equality of the sexes, surely they can perform their bathroom duties without our assistance. We've been told that this is just common courtesy. But if that's the case, then surely it's not a one-way street. How about leaving the toilet seat *up* for us? Don't we deserve a little courtesy too? If women don't want guys to keep peeing on toilet seats, then they should do us all a favor and get them out of our range. But despite the hypocrisy and simplemindedness that exists in the "Toilet Seat Debate," you may just want to go ahead and put the damn things down for them so they'll quit whining about it.

The M Word

You know exactly what we're talking about. The Final Frontier. The Great Beyond. The Fateful Walk Down the Aisle. Countdown to Eternity. It's the big catch that every man wants but doesn't want *now*. It's the culmination of a lifetime of dating and yet also the death of hope. We simultaneously crave it and loathe it, need it and fear it, fall to our knees and beg for it, and then get second thoughts and run away from it. It causes so many mixed emotions in guys that we dare not even speak its name. It starts with an M and ends with an E, and then there are about six letters in between. Don't make us say the word. We're already breaking into a cold sweat just thinking about it.

Sooner or later, most men will be compelled to make the terrifying leap into the unknown and get hitched. We all know it's gonna happen someday, we even want it to happen, but we always think it's gonna happen sometime tomorrow. Like old age, we've accepted the inevitability of its arrival, but we'd be more comfortable if it remained somewhere in our distant future.

The reason for our fear is that few of us have any idea what marriage is really like. We know what happened to our parents, and we certainly don't want to end up like them. We've seen plenty of married couples on TV, but they're all so wildly different and none of them seem very pleasant. The giddy happiness of the Brady Bunch isn't any more appealing to us than the giddy misery of the Bundy Bunch. With so little information to draw on, who could blame us for being unenthusiastic about marriage?

We decided to get the scoop on marriage directly from the source. A good friend of ours—let's call him Bruce—got married not too long ago and, as far as we can tell, he seems to be dealing with it okay. We recently paid him a visit in an attempt to find out exactly what goes on in an honest-to-goodness marriage. Here is what we found:

What Is Marriage Really Like?

Bruce meets us at the door of his three-bedroom condo in sunny Evanston, a prosperous suburb on the northern border of Chicago. Bruce is clean-shaven, energetic, and fully awake on this early Saturday morning. During his bachelor prime, Bruce was known for going weeks without bathing and sleeping well into the afternoon. We are admittedly alarmed to see this one-time king of sloth and late night excess now basking in the glow of the morning sun and, horror upon horrors, even enjoying it. We ask Bruce if marriage is responsible for his newfound appreciation for early rising.

"No, not really," he says. "It has more to do with living in the suburbs. When I was in the city, everybody stayed out late and slept late. But in the 'burbs, everybody is up at the crack of dawn. And when in Rome . . ."

"Why did you move to the suburbs?" we ask. "You still have a job in the city. And there is plenty of urban housing that is just as good as anything you can find out here."

"Yeah, but there aren't many married couples in the city," he says. "They all move out to the suburbs. It's just what you do when you tie the knot. I don't know why it is. I have no reasonable explanation for it. It's not like we were worried about crime or pollution or anything like that. We just felt it was something we had to do. I've talked to other married couples and they all say the same thing. When you get married, you migrate toward the suburbs."

1. You'll probably be living in the suburbs

Bruce takes us on a guided tour of his condo, which he and his lovely wife are in the process of buying. He explains to us that they never even discussed renting a place. They want a home to call their own, something that nobody can take away from them. We point out to him that this also means he will have to take care of all the maintenance on his own. One of the joys of renting is that your landlord is responsible for any major or minor repairs, from fixing a leaking sink to putting in storm windows. Bruce insists that he welcomes the new responsibilities. His coffee table is littered with magazines like *Better Homes and Gardens* and copies of the Time/Life Home Improvement book series. And he enthusiastically tells us about his plans to tear out the floorboards and install brand-new hardwood floors.

"The only thing that has taken some adjustment is decorating," he says. "When I was single, decorating was just throwing some

posters on the wall and buying some sec-
ondhand furniture. Now I have to think
about things like color-coordina-
tion."

"What does that mean?" we
ask.

"In layman's terms, it's basically
about getting colors to match," he says.
"For instance, just last week we went
shopping for a new couch. My first instinct is to
look for a couch that's big enough and comfortable enough.
But then my wife tells me that we also have to find a couch that fits
into the context of the rest of the room."

"You mean, like, it has to look like everything else?"

"Not necessarily. But it has to fit the same mood. The way my
wife explains it, we're decorating the living room in a light blue
'mood.' Everything in the room doesn't have to be light blue, but it
has to mesh with or *suggest* light blue. Some colors work well together, and some colors contradict each other. A couch could be perfect in every other way, but if it doesn't fit into the color scheme that
we've established, then we can't use it."

"That sounds awfully confusing."

"Yeah," Bruce says with a sigh. "It's been hard to get a handle
on."

2. There's a lot of confusing color-coordination involved

Bruce's wife is gone for the day. She's with some of her female
friends at a social function that Bruce doesn't seem to know very
much about. But he says that he's delighted to have the time away
from her.

"I see her all the time," he says. "It's kind of nice to get some
breathing room once in a while, just so we don't get on each other's
nerves."

"Is that a source of a lot of tension?" we ask. "You're pretty much trapped with this woman. It's not like you could just get up and leave her if you ever got sick of the relationship. What do you do to keep your sanity?"

"It's really not that difficult," he says. "I look at it this way. Sure, I'm trapped with her, but she's also trapped with me. When I was just casually dating women, there was always that fear that they could just take off at any moment and there wasn't a damn thing I could do about it. But now I have the security, the peace of mind, that she's pretty much gonna be with me for the long haul."

"What about divorce?" we ask. "That's still a possibility."

"Yeah, of course, but that's more difficult. If you want to divorce someone, you have to get lawyers and do a lot of paperwork and, you know, it's a big pain in the ass. You're only gonna leave someone if you *really* want to leave them. It's not like she's gonna wake up one morning and think, 'This is getting kinda boring. I think I'll leave him.' You know she's gonna put up with a lot more from you because she's too lazy to go through the hassle of dumping you."

3. She's less likely to leave you

Bruce works at the Board of Trade, where he has been an active member since 1991. It's a stressful job with as much chance of devastating financial failure as success. He decided to embark upon this career because he wanted to be self-employed and make his own hours.

"It wasn't a difficult decision for me to make," he says. "I always wanted a career that had an element of excitement and danger to it. This was the most obvious choice for me. But my parents were very upset that I decided to take this road. They wanted me to do something with more security. They're very conservative, and although they can appreciate the financial rewards, they can't stand the fact that I'm gambling with so much of my money. It just doesn't make sense to them."

But then he points to a picture of his parents, posing with Bruce and his wife at their wedding. They're smiling and laughing, looking like the proudest parents in the world. "My marriage changed everything for them," he says. "They still don't like my career, but they feel better now that I have a wife. They might be thinking that she's going to change me or steer me in the right direction. But I also think that parents just like marriage. They want us to follow in their footsteps, and marriage is sometimes the closest thing they can get."

4. It'll make your parents happy

The next stop on our tour was the bedroom, the "Chamber Room of Love" as Bruce describes it. It looks just like what you'd expect from a married couple's bedroom. There are framed oil paintings on the walls, a huge king-size bed covered in fluffy pillows and a hand-woven blanket, and an assortment of antique-looking furniture and collectibles. It is also impeccably clean and organized, with not a single item out of place or sullied in any way.

"Is this really where you sleep or is it just for show?" we ask. "It doesn't look lived-in at all."

"Yeah," Bruce chuckles. "That's the way she likes it. And that's fine by me. I let her do whatever she wants with the bedroom. And she runs a pretty tight ship. If I so much as leave a dirty towel on the floor, she'll bite my head off."

"Doesn't that make you uncomfortable?"

"Oh no, not at all," he says. "I like living in a clean apartment. I just never had the discipline to do it myself. If she wants to take the responsibility of keeping everything in order, she's welcome to it.

And she can decorate it any way she wants to. The only thing I was adamant about was that I didn't want any pictures of relatives in here."

"Why's that?" we ask.

"It's just too weird," he says. "I mean, this is where we have sex. I don't want her grandmother staring at me while I'm having sex with her. That just creeps me out."

We have approached a subject that is of particular interest to us. "What's the sex like?" we ask, tentatively.

"You'd be surprised," he says. "I thought it was going to be different. I thought I'd get bored with it or resentful that I had to have sex with one woman for the rest of my life. But it's not that bad. In all honesty, it's pretty much the same."

"Really? It never seems dull or overly familiar?"

"No, not really. It's the same as it always was. Not any better, but not any worse either."

5. The sex is pretty much the same

We notice a basket full of condoms on an end table next to the bed. "Now that surprises us," we say. "We always thought that one of the advantages of marriage was that you didn't have to use condoms anymore."

"Well, she doesn't want to go on the pill," he says. "And I've never really trusted coitus interruptus. So it's either condoms or, you know . . ."

Bruce's face goes pale and there is an awkward moment of silence.

"Have you talked about kids?" we ask.

Bruce swallows hard and sits on the bed. "Sure, we've talked about it," he says. "You *have* to talk about it. We're married and married people have kids. It's never been a question for us whether we'll have kids. The question is *when*."

"What have you decided?"

"We haven't decided anything. But we're discussing it. That's a big step for me. Before I got married, kids weren't even something I'd *think* about, much less openly discuss with a woman. But things are different now. Even though we haven't made any plans for kids in the near future, the option is always there, hanging over our heads."

Bruce takes us to a small room that, at the moment, is being used as a study. "When we first moved here, we didn't know what to do with this room," he says. "And one day we both came in here and said, almost simultaneously, 'This would make a great nursery.' And it just freaked us out. Actually, it freaked me out a little more, but we were both uncomfortable."

"It scares us and we didn't even say it."

"Exactly. Kids are a big deal, even when you're just casually considering it. And once you've brought them up for the first time, they never go away. You start looking at your entire life in a different way. You start noticing sales on baby clothes, you price private schools. This baby is already a part of our lives and we haven't even had the freaking thing yet."

6. You're that much closer to having kids

Bruce asks us if we want something to drink.

"Sure," we say. "How about a beer?"

"No beer," he says. "All we have is wine."

Bruce gets us some wine and we ask why a one-time professional drunkard like him doesn't have any beer in the house.

"It's not like I quit drinking beer," he says. "We just drink wine more often these days."

"You never used to drink wine," we say. "Why start now?"

"I don't know," he says. "Every couple

we know drinks wine. So we started drinking it too. Maybe it's because it seems more sophisticated or something. It's just something that married people do."

7. Wine becomes your alcoholic beverage of choice

"It sounds like you've been able to adjust fairly well to the changes of married life," we say. "Is there anything about it that bugs you? Any new responsibilities that you can't get used to?"

"Church," he says. "All of a sudden, I have to go to church."

"Dear God, *why?*"

"She says that since we got married in a church, it would be hypocritical of us not to go more often."

"Is it as painful as it sounds?"

"It's worse," he grumbles. "You have to get up early on a Sunday, put on a suit, and sit on a hard pew for an entire hour while some guy in black babbles on at you about sin and redemption. You're uncomfortable and bored and irritated and sleepy. It's just horrible. I hate it."

"So why do you do it?" we ask. "Just tell your wife that you don't want to go."

"It's not that easy. There's a lot of peer pressure among married couples. Most of the married couples in our neighborhood go to church, and if we don't go too, they'd look down on us. All of my wife's friends go to church, and she wants to be part of the community. I just don't understand it though. It's like self-inflicted torture. Why would anybody want to do that to themselves? If there is anything bad about marriage, that would be it."

8. Like it or not, you're going to church

Bruce's wife returns home with an armful of groceries and announces that they will be having guests over for dinner tonight. Bruce just smiles, kisses her, and offers to put away the groceries for her. She disappears and we move to the kitchen.

"Why didn't you ask who these guests are?" we ask.

"Oh, it doesn't matter," he says. "We do this kind of thing all the time. We have probably around two or three dinner parties a week."

"Any reason for that?" we ask. "Are you campaigning for public office or something?"

"It's the married couple's version of a social life," he says. "We don't go to bars or nightclubs anymore. That's strictly for singles. Married people have dinner parties. It's basically the same idea except the music isn't as loud, the food is better, and you're guaranteed to get laid at the end of the night."

As we help Bruce unpack the groceries, we notice that the ma-

jority of the food is cheese. "What's with all the cheese?" we ask. "Is that all you're going to serve tonight?"

"No, that's just for the appetizers. A staple of dinner parties is cheese. Before you sit down for the main course, everybody huddles in the living room and eats cheese. It's the strangest thing I've ever seen."

"Just cheese?"

"Well, sometimes there are crackers, but it's mostly cheese. After helping host a good number of these parties, I've learned more than I ever needed to know about cheese. Before I got married, I thought Cheddar was the only kind of cheese worth paying attention to. But now I know that Cheddar is only the tip of the iceberg."

"Like what, for instance?"

"Well, there's Brie cheese and Stilton cheese and Limburger cheese and Gouda cheese and Bleu cheese."

"Bleu cheese? Isn't that just used in salad dressing?"

"No, some people eat it *as is.*"

"My God!"

"It's actually kind of fascinating. I could probably name fifty kinds of cheese just off the top of my head."

9. You'll learn more than you ever wanted to know about cheese

There is a knock at the door. Bruce opens it to find a scruffy, barely awake vagabond on the other side.

"Hiya, Bruce," the man says. "What's going on?"

"Nothing much," Bruce says, looking somewhat annoyed by the unexpected visitor. The man walks past us and disappears into the kitchen. We ask Bruce who this strange fellow is, and he shakes his head and sighs.

"His name's Henry," he says. "He's an old friend of mine. I've known him since I was a little kid." Bruce moves closer to us and speaks in a whisper. "Actually, I find him kind of irritating these days. But he keeps coming by and hanging out with me like it was old times."

"Why don't you just tell him to get out?" we ask. "If he's such a pain in your ass, you shouldn't have to put up with him. This is your house."

"Yeah, I know," Bruce says. "But still, I feel kinda sorry for him. He doesn't have much else going on in his life. He's thirty years old and he doesn't have a job or any other friends. He hasn't even had a girlfriend that's lasted for more than a few weeks. It's really sad."

We find Henry in the living room, watching TV, and eating a bag of chips. We introduce ourselves to him and explain that we're here investigating marriage for a book.

"Bruce's marriage is a pretty sweet deal," Henry says, loudly munching on his chips. "He's got a nice place and a good little woman who seems to like him okay. I'd say he's done all right for himself."

"What about you?" we ask. "Have you ever thought about getting married?"

"Naw, marriage ain't right for me," he says. "I like my independence too much."

Henry lets out a belch and flicks scraps of potato chips off his belly. "If you ask me, marriage is for suckers," he says. "I don't want a woman around who's gonna boss me around all the time. That really sucks."

"Yeah, but it might be good for you."

"I don't think so," he says. "I think I'm fine just the way I am. If I was looking for self-improvement, I'd be more interested in trying to get my own place."

"Where do you live now?"

"With my parents," he says. "It's cool. The rent's cheap. And, you know, it lets me enjoy the life of a bachelor. That's all I need."

10. Even with all its faults, it's still better than being a pathetic bachelor

We wanted to end this chapter with some words of wisdom from the experts on marriage. Somebody like Marie Kargman, Ann Landers, Regina Barreca, or even our old buddy John "Mars Needs Women" Gray. Unfortunately, we weren't able to track all of them down. Those we contacted refused to speak on the record. For some reason, they were under the impression that we were going to make fun of them in print. But nothing could be further from the truth. We honestly want to know how marriages work and what men should do to make them more successful. Most of the guys we've talked to have no idea what marriage is going to be like in the long run, and it makes them giddy with paranoia and dread. They need reassurance that marriages can indeed survive and might actually be a good idea. But none of them know where to get this information.

After months of searching for some authority on the subject of marriage, we finally realized that we had been barking up the wrong tree. We were trying to get insights from men who were either too young to have any perspective or too immersed in the laboratory environment of touchy-feely marriage workshops to have anything useful to tell us. If we really want to know what marriage is all about, we need to consult men who've had some firsthand experience with it. We need guys who've lived with a woman for twenty, thirty, even fifty years. We need marriage survivors who've seen the highs and lows of a long-term commitment, and who've learned to know exactly what to expect. In short, we need to talk to a bunch of really old guys.

As luck would have it, we found a group of old geezers who were willing to talk to us. They represented a cross section of geriatric America. They were black and white, rich and poor, cognitive and barely conscious. Some of them had been married only once in their lives, and others had been through as many as six wives. But for some reason, which may or may not be relevant, the vast majority of them had the first name "Stan." They were happy, even eager, to tell us everything they knew about the institution of marriage (not to mention a plethora of other subjects too numerous to mention here). And so, without further ado, we give you . . .

Crusty Old Geezers and Their Insights into Marriage

"It's okay. Me and my wife share the same medication, so it's kinda convenient."

"I've been married three times in my life and every time the woman I was with told me to hit the road. They just couldn't put up with me anymore. I'll admit it, I can be a bastard sometimes. But finally I found a woman who's willing to take all my crap. And I love her for it. I think the key to a successful marriage is finding someone who doesn't find you annoying."

"The best reason to get married is that you can count on a woman to carry plenty of gum. Men always want gum, but they never remember to buy it or take it with them. But women always have gum. I never met a woman who didn't have some gum with her. They're good that way."

"The thing you wanna do is find a way to get rid of them when they're bugging you. Whenever my old lady is getting under my skin, I light up a cigar, which she hates the smell of, and I don't hear from her again for the rest of the day. Works like a charm."

"After a while, you just stop talking to her. I stopped talking to my wife fourteen years ago. We get along fine."

"The older you get, you more you need a good snuggling now and again. But not many people want to hug you when you get to be my age. If you've got yourself a good woman, you can get all of the good loving you need."

"Every man needs to be slapped around once in a while. That's what wives are for, to slap their husbands around and keep them in line. Some women are better at slapping around men than others, and those are the ones you wanna marry."

"I've never been married, and I'll tell you why. I don't like old women. Their boobs sag, their butts get bigger, their entire body goes straight to hell. I say no thank you to that. Who needs it? I'd rather play chess all day than help her into her goddamn corset. It makes me sick just thinking about it. I'm done talking to you."

"My marriage still works because we've kept the sex interesting. We do all kinds of things. We dress up, we fool around in public places, we got all sorts of sex toys. When I feel like my marriage is getting dull, I just ask my wife to put on her sexy little French maid outfit and I feel much better."

"I got only one word of advice: Do whatever she says to do. Don't get your own ideas on how a marriage is supposed to work. We don't know anything about it and we don't wanna know nothing neither. Just let her do the talking and you do what you're told and everything will be super."

"A wife is good for making you food and making sure you have plenty of clean underwear. Without my wife around, I'd be a hungry fool with one pair of shorts. And who needs that?"

"The best thing about marriage is you always have someone to look out for you. If you get sick, she'll put you in bed and make you soup. If you get drunk and end up in jail, she'll bail you out and sober you up. If some guy shoots you in the nuts and you gotta go to the hospital, she'll be there to pick you up and pay the bill. And then when you keel over and die, she'll make sure you get buried okay and get a nice-looking casket."

"Marriage is a big ol' pain in the ass. But what the hell else are ya gonna do with your life?"

Acknowledgements

Foremost, we thank Bruce Tracy, our editor and "love pump" at Doubleday. We still fondly remember the many nights we spent in his office debating the rules of dating, getting into wild, uninhibited tickle fights, and laughing like schoolgirls. Oh, the fun we had. We also give thanks to Jane and Danielle, our deadly brace of agents.

Brendan acknowledges the genetic and artistic debt he owes his amorphous, ever-expanding family. He'd also like to thank every person who, willingly or not, provided raw material for this book. Extra thanks go to Ray Pride's acute eyesight and Michael Cook's timely advice on gayness. Invaluable advice from Milissa Deitz, Tracey Pepper, and Krista Roslof was greatly appreciated, if mostly ignored. Brendan would thank all of the magazine editors he's ever worked for, but he's certain some of the cheap bastards still owe him money.

Spitznagel thanks his family (Ma, Pa, Bro, and Grams), who supported him through poverty and near-poverty, never once telling him to "get a real job." Thanks are also due to the silly little bitches at Second City, who have been like a second family to him. In particular, he thanks T. J. Jagodoski for the tough love, Bret Scott for the computer assistance, and Matty Cullison for the hugs. Special thanks to "Babs" Kreglow and Michael Grollman for giving him the best publicity that money didn't buy, and Merle Grollman because her brother wouldn't thank her in his book. And, of course, he thanks Kelly Kreglow, his partner in all things and the funniest woman alive. Her inspiration and devotion have kept this boy from becoming a bitter old cynic.

And last but not least, we give thanks to all of our ex-girlfriends, who are (in no particular order) Katie, Stephanie, Susan, Heather, Claire, Becky, Chrissy, Debbie, Fleur, Julie, Emily, Renée, Caroline, Nadia, Ensley, Heidi, Kat, and every tedious variation on "Jennifer" (i.e., Jen, Jenny, Jenna, etcetera). Without you ladies, we would have nothing funny to say about dating.

Index

Printed in the United States
by Baker & Taylor Publisher Services